The Art of Writing Advertising

The Art of Writing Advertising

Conversations with

WILLIAM BERNBACH

LEO BURNETT

GEORGE GRIBBIN

DAVID OGILVY

ROSSER REEVES

Interviewed by Denis Higgins

NTC Business Books
NTC/Contemporary Publishing Company

Library of Congress Cataloging-in-Publication Data
is available from the United States Library of Congress.

Published by NTC Business Books
An imprint of NTC/Contemporary Publishing Company
4255 West Touhy Avenue, Lincolnwood (Chicago), Illinois 60646-1975 U.S.A.

Printed in the United States of America
International Standard Book Number: 0-8442-3100-2
23 22 21 20 19 18 17 16 15 14 13 12 11 10 9 8 7

Contents

INTRODUCTION . . . . 8 *Page*

WILLIAM BERNBACH 10

LEO BURNETT 26

GEORGE GRIBBIN 48

DAVID OGILVY 70

ROSSER REEVES 94

Introduction

FOR MOST PEOPLE writing is a lonely, frustrating and sometimes unhappy experience. The writer who actually enjoys the process of writing seems to be unusual; most writers enjoy *having written* but get no joy whatever from the actual task of moving a pencil across a sheet of paper or hitting one key after another on a typewriter.

Buckling down to the task of writing is a sort of horror, to be put off until the last possible minute. An infinitely complicated and pointless ritual, much like the contortions a baseball pitcher frequently goes through before he finally cocks his arm and actually starts the pitching motion, is often involved. Paper must be stacked just so; the typewriter or the pencils must be fingered, caressed, carefully lined up. Coffee must be drunk, or not drunk. The window must be opened, closed or adjusted. The chair must be raised, lowered, moved in, moved out, or replaced. That new, funny looking spot on the neck must be carefully inspected in the bathroom mirror; or the girl whose profile shows in the window across the business canyon must be speculatively regarded. Time moves on, and so does the pointless ritual, until at last the moment can no longer be postponed. It is time to *start writing* . . .

It was the intimate knowledge of this sort of harrowing experience that was in the mind of James Vincent O'Gara, executive editor of Advertising Age, when he suggested one day to senior editor Denis Higgins that he interview the five "advertising greats" who had thus far been elected to the New York Copywriters Hall of Fame.

"The essence of this business is putting effective words and phrases down on paper," he said. "And practically every writer of advertising, like every writer of anything else, goes through these horrible gyrations on his way to turning out a page of print copy, or a television commercial, or a set of instructions on how to assemble Widget A without losing either your patience or your thumb. Talk to these great and successful writers of advertising about this mundane but important matter of how they prepare themselves to get at it. See if they have developed any little gimmicks for getting the productive juices to flow more freely. Ask them if they have learned anything in their rich experience which might help other aspiring writers to get there faster with less frustration and, perhaps, somewhat better results."

So Denis Higgins hunted down his five hero-victims, armed with tape recorder, a fistful of questions (some of them innocuous) and an inquiring and somewhat unconventional mind.

What emerged from these sessions is what appears in this book. Far from developing into a pedantic discussion of how to sharpen pencils before sitting down to write, Higgins' victims gave forth, under his prodding, with some of the most interesting discussions on the writing of advertising which it has ever been my privilege to see.

When these discussions were published in the Feature Section of Advertising Age, they created tremendous interest, along with innumerable requests for their reproduction in permanent form.

To the reader who has any interest at all in advertising, in advertising writing, or indeed in writing or expression of any kind, the five interviews in this volume are certain to be of absorbing interest. Here are masters of their craft, talking—not writing—informally, freely and cogently, about their craft, their skills, their ideas, their notions and their ideals. Let's join the conversation . . .

S. R. Bernstein
Publisher, Advertising Age

*"One of the problems [is] worship of research.
We're all concerned about the facts we get, and not enough concerned about how provocative we make them to consumers."*

William Bernbach

In a recording studio in the offices of Doyle Dane Bernbach on New York's 43rd St. sits William Bernbach. He is smaller than one expects, soft spoken, conservatively suited. He sits on a folding chair, back to a battered piano, regarding the interviewer in the manner of an innocent man being grilled by an auditor from the Internal Revenue Service. The interview begins . . .

Q. *Mr. Bernbach, how did you get into writing advertising copy?*

A. Well, actually, I used to ghost speeches for a lot of famous people—for governors, mayors, a lot of prominent people. And I had an interest in art. I think the combination of writing and art led to an integration of graphics and copy that made for a perhaps more efficient use of the total medium of advertising.

Q. *Going back before that, even, what I wanted to ask you was, what made you decide you wanted to get into this business? Into writing?*

A. Well, I think we're getting too precise. I don't think that everything is measured by definite decisions—on one day when suddenly I was going into advertising. I don't know how that happened. It just gradually happened. I was interested in writing. I was interested in art, and when the opportunity came along to do writing and art in advertising, I just took the opportunity. Directly before I went into an advertising agency, I worked at the old New York World's Fair.

Q. *In 1939?*

A. That was in 1939. I was in charge of the literary department—we called it the research department. We wrote for the Encyclopaedia

Brittanica on the history of fairs; we wrote many articles for various publications and I worked on some of the art end for the fair. And after the fair was over, someone had told an agency man about me. He asked me to come down and see him, and I did, and I was challenged by the opportunity to get into advertising. . .

Q. *Who was the man?*

A. The man was William H. Weintraub. And I competed for a job there with many veterans of the advertising business, and got the job on the basis of some writing I was asked to do by Mr. Weintraub. Which I think, maybe, is proof of a position I hold today. I wouldn't go for too routinized men in my copy department. I pull 'em in from all over the lot. I think it tends to give a fresh point of view, an outside point of view. And what there is to know about advertising, we teach them later.

Q. *That touches on one of the questions I wanted to ask you. Do you think writing ad copy is more difficult than writing other kinds of factual copy?*

A. No. I think it takes a discipline, with a knowledge of advertising and what you're trying to accomplish. Learning what you're trying to accomplish comes later. I think the first and most important thing in advertising is to be original and fresh. Do you know that 85% of the ads *don't* get looked at? This is a statistic gathered by people commissioned by the advertising business. By the Harvard

IN BERNBACH MANNER—*One of many Ohrbach ads written by Mr. Bernbach himself, this one follows the writer's demand that each ad be fresh and original: "One of the disadvantages of doing everything mathematically, by research, is that after a while, everybody does it the same way . . . If you take the attitude that once you have found out what to say, your job is done, then what you're doing is saying it the same way as everybody is saying it, and you've lost your impact completely."*

IBERAL TRADE-IN
bring in your wife
and just a few dollars
we will give you a new woman
Ohrbach's
"A BUSINESS IN MILLIONS ...
A PROFIT IN PENNIES"

Business School. And we tried to find out what people think of advertising. We wondered whether the advertising community was loved by the American people. We're not even hated! They ignore us. So the most important thing as far as I'm concerned is to be fresh, to be original—to be able to compete with all the shocking news events in the world today, with all the violence. Because you can have all the right things in an ad, and if nobody is made to stop and listen to you, you've wasted it. And we in America are spending so darn much money for efficiency, to measure things, that we're achieving boredom like we've never achieved before. We're *right* about everything, but nobody looks.

Q. *Getting back to copywriting. You say you want writers from all over. What kinds of writers do you look for?*

A. Well, I don't look for writers according to the specific job . . .

Q. *Let me rephrase that: You've had many writers working for you in your time. Have you discerned any striking characteristics about any of them—the more talented or creative people?*

A. I think I have said before, and I'm going to repeat it to you now. One of the problems here is that we're looking for a formula. What makes a good writer? It's a danger. It's this attitude that makes for poor writers. It makes for people trying to be writers who shouldn't be writers.

I remember those old *Times* interviews where the interviewer would talk to the novelist or short story writer, and say, "What time do you get up in the morning? What do you have for breakfast? What time do you start work? When do you stop work? . . ." And the whole implication is that if you eat corn flakes at 6:30 in the morning, and then take a walk and then take a nap and then start working and then stop at noon, you, too, can be a great writer.

You can't be that mathematical and that precise. This business of trying to measure everything in precise terms is one of the problems with advertising today. This leads to a worship of research.

We're all concerned about the facts we get, and not enough concerned about how provocative we make those facts to the consumer.

Q. *Mr. Bernbach, people who write do have certain ways of accumulating ideas and maybe storing them away for some future time. In your time you have had lots of striking ideas, and I wondered if you find it easier to write with ground rules established by the client—you have to have a picture of something, and have to write to it—or do you find it easier to write when you have carte blanche?*

A. We don't permit any client to give us ground rules. We think it's bad for the client. Look, let me put it this way. We think we will never know as much about a product as a client. After all, he sleeps and breathes his product. He's built it. He's lived with it most of his life. We couldn't possibly know as much about it as he does. By the same token, we firmly believe that he can't know as much about advertising. Because *we* live and breathe *that* all day long. And the fact that we're handling the same product has nothing to do with that.

We require a different set of skills from his. He requires skills to make and market that product and we require skills that can provoke and persuade the consumer. They're two different things, entirely different things. And one of the disadvantages of doing everything mathematically, by research and by mandate, is that after a while, everybody does it in the same way. Because you go out and find out the same things—and if you take the attitude, as many people do, that once you have found out what to say, your job is done, then what you're doing is saying it the same way as everybody is saying it, and then you've lost your impact completely.

Q. *What we're talking about, Mr. Bernbach, is from the individual's point of view, rather than the industry's point of view. Now, there are lots of people in the advertising business who are writers, per-*

"A very, very big prospect once said to me, 'What would you say, Bill, if you were told exactly where to put the logo and what size it would be.' I had $10,000,000 riding on my answer, and I said, 'I would say we are the wrong agency for you'."

haps not-so-good writers, but writers who want to be better writers. What we're trying to get out of this is not formulas, or precise theories about how you go about being a better copywriter; what we're trying to get from you, a veteran in this business who has demonstrated his ability as a copywriter, is what these writers can do to improve their own skills.

A. Well, I wish I could give them an equation, so that all they have to do is follow it. But I can't. What they have to do is keep working, keep thinking, keep being as honest as they can about what they're doing, keep practicing . . . I know these are bromides, but to go beyond that would be trying to fool you.

Q. *Well, I've asked other people what outside sources they use, what interests they pursue, to keep their points of view fresh. Could you answer me that one?*

A. Well, I do a lot of reading, if that's one of the things you mean.

Q. *Yes. In what fields?*

A. I do a great deal of reading in philosophy. I do a great deal of reading in fiction. I'm sure that everything a man does is grist for his copy mill. I'm sure of that—what you've done and what you've experienced—if you can put more thinking and more interesting things into your copy, you're that much more provocative.

Q. *How much do you write now? Do you write frequently?*

A. Well, today I don't do much body copy any more, at all. But I edit almost everything in the shop. And I still conceive headlines for ads. Let me make one important point: There's an old saying—it's certainly not mine, but I subscribe to it completely—that you write better when you have something to write about. And if I gave any advice to anybody, it's to know his product inside out before he starts working. Your cleverness, your provocativeness and imagination and inventiveness must stem from knowledge of the product. I think the worst thing that's happening today is this juggling of a page of graphics—it's not hard for anybody to get ideas—the important thing is to recognize when the idea is good. You must have imagination, you must have inventiveness, but it must be disciplined. Everything you write, everything on a page, every word, every graphic symbol, every shadow, should further the message you're trying to convey. You know, you measure the success of any work of art by how well it's achieved its purpose.

And anybody in advertising who doesn't say his purpose is to sell that piece of merchandise is a phony. And you must be as simple, and as swift, and as penetrating as possible. And it must stem from knowledge. And you must relate that knowledge to the consumer's needs. I don't say that by being imaginative that you just go out and be cute. I have very often given the example of being able to attract people to an ad by standing a man on his head on a page. But that is not a good ad unless you're selling a product that keeps things from falling out of that man's pockets. *Then* your inventiveness, and your attractiveness, and your cleverness is furthering, and making memorable, the advantage of your product.

If you don't do things this way, well, No. 1, you haven't attracted people to your page, and therefore you've wasted money, no matter what you say in your ad. If you do that, and it doesn't relate to your product, then you've created resentment because people feel they've been tricked into reading about your product. What you must do, by the most economical and creative means possible, is attract people and sell them. Now, this is difficult. This is sweat. This is working.

Q. *I wanted to ask you briefly about your own habits . . .*

A. (Laughter.)

Q. *Why are you laughing?*

A. I'm laughing because you are going to habits again as if that were the answer.

Q. *No, it's not the answer. I realize it's not the answer.*

A. I have almost 100 people in copy around here and I doubt if two have the same habits. And yet they're tremendous.

Q. *What I mean by habits—when you did write body copy, were you your own editor, even though you were the boss?*

A. Yes, sure. Absolutely.

Q. *And you don't need an outsider, a third man to edit you?*

A. One of the advantages I feel and one of the things I am very proud of in this shop is that as president of this agency I am a creative man. And if I'm going over my copywriters' work, it's as somebody who has been doing what they're trying to do now. It's someone who knows their problems. It's someone who has been through it. It's someone who has had that experience. I'm not just a business man holding a yoke over them and imposing on them. As a matter of fact, even though I feel I know this business, I don't impose my personality on them even now. What I try to find out is what their particular talent is and nourish that.

That's why I think we have the wonderful depth of talent in this organization. And the wonderful range and variety of talent. Because we have not imposed our kind of talent on our people. We have rather searched for what is outstanding. For example, I have one man who is tremendous in humor, just has a natural feeling for humor. One is very swift and straight and piercing and goes right to the heart of the problem. They're all different people. Each one's personality makes for effective work. Now it would be wrong for me to make the man who is great at humor do something he can't do. This is the important thing. You have to find out what their talent is and nurture that, because that's a natural thing. Instead of trying to make everybody do exactly the same thing and winding up boring everybody.

"We tried to find out what people think of advertising . . . whether the advertising community was loved by the American people. We're not even hated! They ignore us. So the most important thing as far as I'm concerned is to be fresh, to be original."

Q. *You seem to feel that there are people in the business now who impose personalities, either the agency's or their own, on writers.*

A. Don't misunderstand me. I respect many agencies in the business. But this is our way of working: Not to regiment; not to have too many rules.

Q. *What about disciplines? There is a difference between rules and disciplines?*

A. Yes. My discipline—all I want is for the idea to convey memorably (and because it's memorable, it must be fresh and original) the advantage of our product. Now if breaking every rule in the world is going to achieve that, I want those rules broken. I don't want to say to my creative team, "Put a picture on top, put in a headline and then put copy underneath." On the other hand, I don't want to say, "Don't do that." But there will be a time when no headline is proper, there will be a time when a headline is proper. There will be a time when a logo is good and there will be a time when using a logo is the worst thing in the world you can do.

You want an example of that? Suppose I have a product that does not have a good reputation with a consumer. Well, a logo is like a man's name. When I mention a certain man you know well, everything about that man jumps into your mind. It conjures up what that man is. A logo does the same thing for a product. Now

'DEEP AFFECTION'—*Says Mr. Bernbach of this and other noted ads he has written for this client: "I started with the Ohrbach campaign myself, and I did the Ohrbach ads personally for about 17 years running; so I have a deep affection for them." Adding that he lately attended Mr. Ohrbach's 79th birthday celebration, he commented: "I think of that as more than just an account."*

I found out
about
Joan
e way she talks, you'd think she was in Who's Who. Well! found out what's what with *her*. Her husband own a nk? Sweetie, not even a bank *account*. Why that palace theirs has wall-to-wall *rtgages!* And that car? rling, that's horsepower, t earning power. They won it in a fifty-cent raffle! Can you imagine? And those clothes! Of course she *does* dress divinely. But really…a mink stole, and Paris suits, and all those dresses…on *his* income? Well darling, I found out about that too. I just happened to be going her way and *I saw Joan come out of Ohrbach's!*
Ohrbach's
TH ST. OPP. EMPIRE STATE BLDG. • NEWARK MARKET & HALSEY • "A BUSINESS IN MILLIONS, A PROFIT IN PENNIES"™

EATING IT UP—*This ad was conceived and written by Mr. Bernbach, who said: "You must have inventiveness, but it must be disciplined. Everything you write, everything on a page, every word, every graphic symbol, every shadow, should further the message you're trying to convey."*

suppose my product is not in good standing with the consumer and I have a very big name on the page. The consumer sees that name and he feels he knows everything about that product and he turns the page. And I've lost him.

But if I put down a very intriguing thought and that's the first thing he sees, and then I lead him from that intriguing thought to certain factual things, and then at the end say, "This is what our product is now," I've held him and I've convinced him. And this becomes a very, very important fact. So just to say, "Always have a logo," is wrong. As a matter of fact, I can tell you that a very, very big prospect once said to me, "What would you say, Bill, if you were told exactly where to put the logo and what size it would be." I had over $10,000,000 riding on my answer, and I said, "I would say we are the wrong agency for you." Now, in the long run I think this makes for a very healthy agency because we preserve our point of view. It lets us do the kind of creative work we really believe in and not prostitute that talent for that 15%. Because, as I say, in the long run the client forgets how he told you to do something. He only remembers whether it worked or not.

Q. *Probably everybody is influenced at one time or another by individuals or things. Have you had any influences in your life as a copywriter?*

A. I'm sure I've had many. I was once a music student, and I had a very wonderful music teacher with a powerful personality. I am sure that, while I was growing up and undergoing that instruction, it molded a point of view. You know, you are a result of all the forces that ever came to play on you and I can't sit down now and say that one was the great influence. It's just the sum of all those things.

I want to say further that I think the most important element in success in ad writing is the product itself. And I can't say that often enough. Or emphasize it enough. Because I think a great ad campaign will make a bad product fail faster. It will get more people to know it's bad. And it's the product itself that's all important and that's why we, as an agency, work so closely with the client on his product—looking for improvements, looking for ways to make people want it, looking for additions to the product, looking for changes in the product. Because when you have that, you are giving the people something that they can't get elsewhere. And that is fundamentally what sells. Now if you add to that a very skillful way of conveying that advantage, you're ahead of the game. But no matter how skillful you are, you can't invent an advantage that doesn't exist. And if you do, and it's just a gimmick, it's going to fall apart, anyway.

So we never kid ourselves about the magic of advertising. The magic is in the product. And that's why we think clients are so very important; we think we are very fortunate with the clients we have. And I want to add further, we don't care who makes that ad better. If a client says to use something we never thought of and it makes that a better ad, we more than welcome it. We're not arbitrary, at all. We just want the greatest possible ad. Because in the long run that's what counts. You sell merchandise and everybody's happy; you could have the greatest service in the world and if that merchandise doesn't sell, there's going to be dissatisfaction.

Q. *You've answered this question, but let me ask it, anyway. Many ad writers, particularly people who have been extraordinarily successful, dislike writing about certain kinds of products on the grounds that they simply don't like the kinds of products that they write about. Do you feel that way about any product?*

A. Yes, you know . . .

Q. *Cigarets?*

A. Cigaret advertising.

Q. *How about from the point of view of writing? Simply writing about the product? As against the qualities of the product.*

A. Well, I fundamentally believe that what you think about something affects your writing. You know we had the Johnson campaign because we believe; we would not have taken the opposite side. No matter how much money was involved, we would not have taken it. What you believe, if you believe in something deeply, and you know it, is going to come across even if you don't have the skills your competition has. Now if you can combine skill with a deep belief, you're 'way ahead of the game.

Q. *Mr. Bernbach, among the ads you have turned out through the years, which is your favorite?*

A. Well, you know I started with the Ohrbach campaign myself. And I did the Ohrbach ads personally for about 17 years running. So I have a deep affection for them. I did the cat ad, for example. You know the one I mean. I attended Mr. Ohrbach's 79th birthday celebration the other day. He was our first account and there's a very deep relationship there. I must say that I think of that as more than just an account, and I have a deep feeling for it.

Q. *Just let me ask you a "reporter-at-the-railroad-station-question," and I ask it because I have asked it of everybody else in the Copywriters Hall of Fame. If you have a son and he wants to go into the business of copywriting, what would you tell him?*

A. I would tell him everything I just finished telling you.

Leo Burnett

"If you don't get noticed, you don't have anything. You just have to be noticed, but the art is in getting noticed naturally, without screaming or without tricks."

A grey day in New York. It is ten o'clock in the morning and Leo Burnett, looking like a prosperous Rotarian from out-of-town, perhaps a well-to-do tractor dealer from the Plains States, maintains gruffly that he doesn't like these damned tape recorders. "I'm a writer, not a public speaker," he says. He moves around his suite in the Plaza Hotel and gazes out a window at a deserted Central Park. It is winter and it has been snowing and the agency man's mood is as blustery as the weather outside. "Well," he says, taking a seat in an armchair by the window. "Well, hell, plug the damn thing in, and let's get started . . . "

Q. *How did you get started in the business—what made you want to get into the newspaper business or into the advertising business?*

A. Well, I never dreamed I was ever going into the advertising business. We lived in a small town; I was practically brought up under a printing press. I started in as a printer's devil and learned to set type and had my own little press at home. I would print little things. I took pied type home with me from the barrel at the newspaper shop, and sorted it out, and had my own case of type at home.

Q. *You were more interested in the technical end of the business—printing?*

A. Well, no, they sent me down to the station to see who was coming in, who was leaving; and I used to chase all over the county on my bicycle—for obituaries—and started writing little stories for the newspaper at a very early age. And when I was in school, I worked during the summers at a newspaper. So I always thought I was going to be a newspaper man.

"[Working as a reporter,] I learned a lot from newspapers as to how to communicate and how to put color into copy. But finding the magic things to say about a product that would interest people and lead them by the hand to the conclusion that they should buy something—that was another art, really."

Q. *Was your dad in the business?*

A. No, my dad was at a dry goods store—which I hated, but he was very tolerant of my inclinations toward the newspaper business. And so I didn't spend much time in the dry goods store. I played around. I married a woman whose father had been a newspaper man. And went to school and studied all the journalism they had in those days at the University of Michigan.

Q. *They didn't have much journalism in school?*

A. Oh, not in a formal way, but we had some very knowledgeable professors, one of whom was a particular influence, Dr. Fred Newton Scott. And he encouraged all of us to subscribe to the *New York World,* which in those days was a brilliantly written newspaper. This was back in 1911, 1912, 1913—along in there.

Q. *Yes, great staff, wasn't it?*

A. It was a brilliant paper where Heywood Broun and a lot of top writers were working . . . Their writings and Franklin P. Adams' column, "The Conning Tower," was running in those days. And so I read the *New York World* every day and studied the style. And I started in trying to write short stories—would sell one once in a while. And so right after my graduation—that summer after my graduation—I worked as editor of the *Michigan Wolverine;* the summer paper for the University. I got 300 bucks for that—which was pretty big money in 1914. And after that, after the summer school was over, I intended to come to New York and say to the *New York World,* give me a job as a reporter! And I was all steamed up and the *New York World* didn't know what they had coming.

But I was walking across the campus one Saturday afternoon and I ran into a friend of mine who was back to cover the early sport news, the football training stories. He was sports correspondent for some Detroit and Chicago papers—his name was T. Hawley Tapping. So I just happened to run into Tap on the campus on my way home, and he asked me what I was going to do. I told him

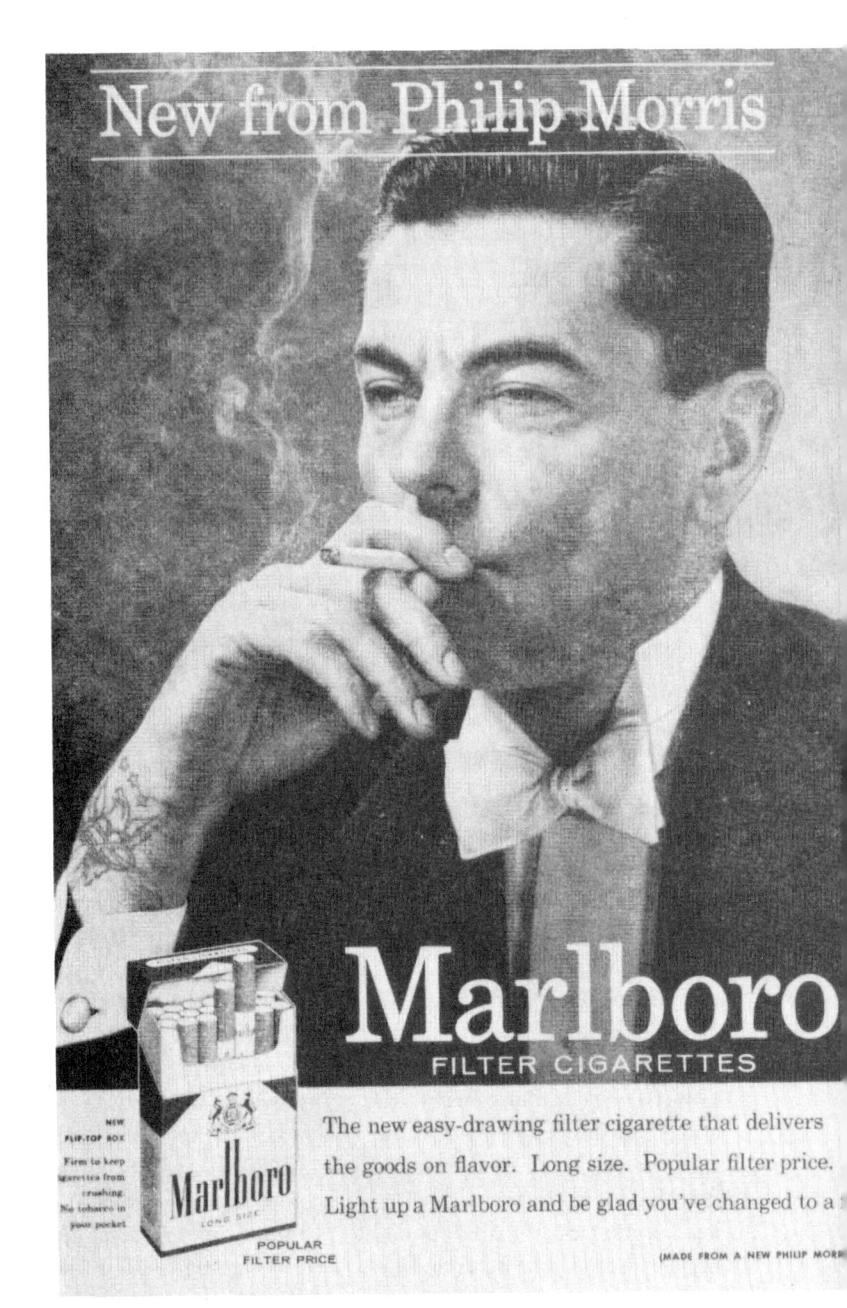
New from Philip Morris
Marlboro
FILTER CIGARETTES
NEW
FLIP-TOP BOX
Firm to keep
garettes from
crushing.
No tobacco in
your pocket
Marlboro
LONG SIZE
POPULAR
FILTER PRICE
The new easy-drawing filter cigarette that delivers
the goods on flavor. Long size. Popular filter price.
Light up a Marlboro and be glad you've changed to a
(MADE FROM A NEW PHILIP MORR

I was going to New York and get a job on the *New York World*. "Don't be silly," he said, "I just came from Peoria yesterday." He'd been brought up on a Peoria newspaper, the *Peoria Journal*. And he said, "There's a job open down there, and you'd get 18 bucks a week. Don't be silly and go to New York, because on a paper the size of the *Journal* you can cover all the bases and this is a hot little paper and a wonderful editor."

Anyway, George Fitch, who wrote the Siwash stories for *The Saturday Evening Post*, which was popular in those days, had been editor of it and was still connected with it. And that appealed to me a little bit, because I had read his stories. But I didn't think much of the job, so I said I was going to New York, anyway, and thanked him. And, well, Sunday morning he called me at home and said: "They're expecting you to report at the *Peoria Journal* at seven o'clock Monday morning—tomorrow morning."

Q. *He applied for the job for you?*

A. Yes, he had paid no attention to my indifference to his suggestion. And so I said, what the hell, this is a job and I got to thinking it over, and it was probably the cowardly thing to do, but anyway, there I was. And so I got on a Michigan Central train and went to Chicago. That was the first time I had ever been to Chicago. And I got on the train and went to Peoria that night with an old, battered-up suitcase. I went directly from the station to the *Peoria Journal*, not knowing where I was going to live.

TATTOO MAN—*In the notable campaign of Leo Burnett and staff for Marlboro, the first ad pictured a cowboy. This one—No. 2—still depicts the masculine (with the now-famous tatoo), but in white tie and tails. Says Mr. Burnett: "I think [our effort] typifies the Chicago school of advertising . . . we try to be more straightforward without being flatfooted. We try to be warm without being mawkish."*

Q. *With your suitcase in hand?*

A. With my suitcase . . . and I walked in the city room and the city editor barely shook hands with me. He said, "Your desk is over there." And then, "Get up to the city hall and see what's going on."

Q. *You didn't even have to fill out a form? . . .*

A. No, no—and so I folded up some copy paper and stuck it in my pocket and went up to the city hall—I didn't even know where that was, of course. Peoria was a pretty rough town in those days; it was a distillery town and a river town and pretty rough. So I first encountered a big cage of weekend drunks who were all trying to get my attention to send messages to somebody. I knew enough not to get trapped into that. But I went in and started nosing around, and got a story about a guy who had killed his wife with an ice-pick over the weekend—and I got the dope on that. I knew enough—I'd written a lot of newspaper stories—how to put a story together, how to get the facts.

Then I met the reporter for the rival paper, the *Peoria Star*. He was very nice to me and introduced me around to everybody I should meet. I got two or three other little items, and I got back to the office and wrote this stuff. And I thought I was all through around noon. Of course, it was an evening paper and they were "closed" around noon, you know. Then the city editor, who was sort of a tyrant, said: "Now, go out and cover the railroads."

Q. *This was while your suitcase was still in the office . . .*

A. The suitcase was still in the office—and I said: "How do you do that (cover the railroads)?" Well, Peoria in those days was quite a railroad town and a lot of railroads came through there. He said: "Well, go around and get acquainted with the passenger agents and the freight agents and stuff." So I started making the rounds of the railroads.

In the meantime, as I worked on the paper I was in correspondence with a classmate of mine from Michigan by the name of

Owen B. Winters who, as you know, later became quite a famous advertising man . . . at Erwin Wasey. Obie, following graduation, had gone to Detroit and got himself a job, first, at Packard Motor Car Co. (which was the big thing then, a big fine-car manufacturer, tops in that field) to edit their magazine. The Detroit Athletic Club was relatively new in those days, and they had a publication called "The DAC News." And Obie got on the staff of that. And he started getting mixed up in things in Detroit in the automotive end of

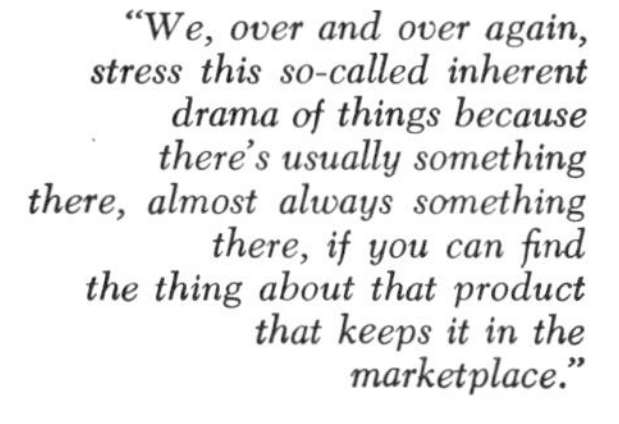

"We, over and over again, stress this so-called inherent drama of things because there's usually something there, almost always something there, if you can find the thing about that product that keeps it in the marketplace."

things—quite importantly. And they were paying him a handsome salary: I believe he started at $40 a week—compared to my $18.

He wrote me that I was a sucker to stay in Peoria, that the automobile business was here to stay. And this was, you see, in 1915. And so, just for the hell of it—just about the same kind of circumstance as meeting Tap on the campus that afternoon—I wrote a letter to Fred Newton Scott, who had been my favorite English professor at Michigan. I told him that I'd heard that sometimes companies wrote to universities looking for people, looking for talent, and that I was kind of interested in looking into something in Detroit. Well, I really didn't think anything would come of it. But I got a wire from him that the Cadillac Motor Car Co. was looking for a man to write a house magazine . . .

Q. *Excellent timing . . .*

A. The timing was excellent, the timing was really something. I followed up on that over the course of the following few weeks. One thing led to another. Negotiations went on over a period of several weeks, but I think at Cadillac they tried to kiss me off—because they didn't like my looks very well. I suspected this because the man I talked to, who later became my boss, a wonderful man by the name of Earle Howard, asked me to go back and write an essay on neatness.

He told me the story of some Cadillac dealer who made a great thing of good housekeeping in his dealer-establishment and keeping his windows clean and all that kind of business—the importance of good housekeeping and neatness in running an automobile dealership. Well, that seemed like kind of a fuzzy assignment. But I went back to Peoria and started writing about neatness.

I went up to see the Cadillac dealer in Peoria, and I wrote a lot of stuff. And I went to the stationery shop there in Peoria and bought the thickest, best quality paper that they had; and on my own Underwood in my room at the YMCA—after I finally got this thing together—I typed it about as neatly as anything could possibly be typed with nice wide margins on it. And sent it up to Detroit. Before I sent it, however, I showed it to George Fitch and got a little guidance on it—this didn't do any harm. He edited it a little bit. But, anyway, I got the job, and went to Detroit.

Q. *And from there . . . you got in on . . . ?*

A. Then I went to Detroit, editing this house magazine. As things developed, I got into the advertising end of it and finally was put in charge of advertising at Cadillac. In the course of that, I got quite well acquainted with Theodore MacManus, who wrote the famous "The Penalty of Leadership" ad, which had been written just before I went to Cadillac.

T. F. MacManus was one of the great advertising men of all time. I was fortunate to be able to spend quite a lot of time with him, and I became fascinated with his thinking and his quality-mindedness and his great power of assumptiveness that he employed in his copy. He really put Cadillac on the map. It was a fine car, but Packard was tops . . .

Q. *All the undertakers used Packards, as I recall . . . they did when I was a boy, anyway . . .*

A. Well, I don't know that they did, because one of my jobs in the early days at Cadillac was to prepare literature for chassis for hearses—special chassis they had for hearses—and I studied up on that and subscribed to *Sunnyside*, the "official organ" of the undertaking establishments. So I became quite familiar with the undertaking trade—and I don't know—we sold a lot of hearses, I know that . . .

Then, World War I was in progress, and I was in the Navy for a short time—never got to sea; I spent most of my time at Great Lakes, building a breakwater up there, hauling cement.

Q. *When you went from the editorial side into the advertising side, did you find that your newspaper experience was helpful to you?*

A. Yes, it was most helpful, because I think it taught me the importance of curiosity about things. I didn't know beans about automobiles, but I became very curious about what made a motor run and all about it. I wrote a lot of fairly technical stuff in a popular way.

Well, after the war,I went back to Cadillac. And then LaFayette Motors Co. was formed by some people at Cadillac, including the man who hired me. They were going to be the American Rolls-Royce—a great idea, but they ran into the depression of 1921.

They moved to Indianapolis, and I went along as advertising manager. But they ran into trouble with this car in an economic dip at that time. And I could see the handwriting on the wall . . . Charles W. Nash was connected with it. They talked about moving it to Racine and Kenosha, which I didn't like very well, since I had established myself in Indianapolis.

Then I got an offer from Homer McKee who was head of the top agency in Indianapolis in those days. So I grabbed it. That was my first agency job. I left LaFayette and went to work for McKee as head of his creative operation. He was a great copywriter, himself, and I learned a lot from him.

Q. *Well, one of the things I wanted to ask you, Mr. Burnett—touching on what you've said—did you find writing ad copy more difficult than writing newspaper copy?*

A. Much more difficult, yes, because it has to be so much more compact and yet it has to deliver the facts, too. I learned a lot from newspapers as to how to communicate and how to put color and interest into advertising copy. But finding the magic things to say about a product that would interest people and evoke their interest and lead them by the hand to the conclusion that they should buy something—that was another art, really.

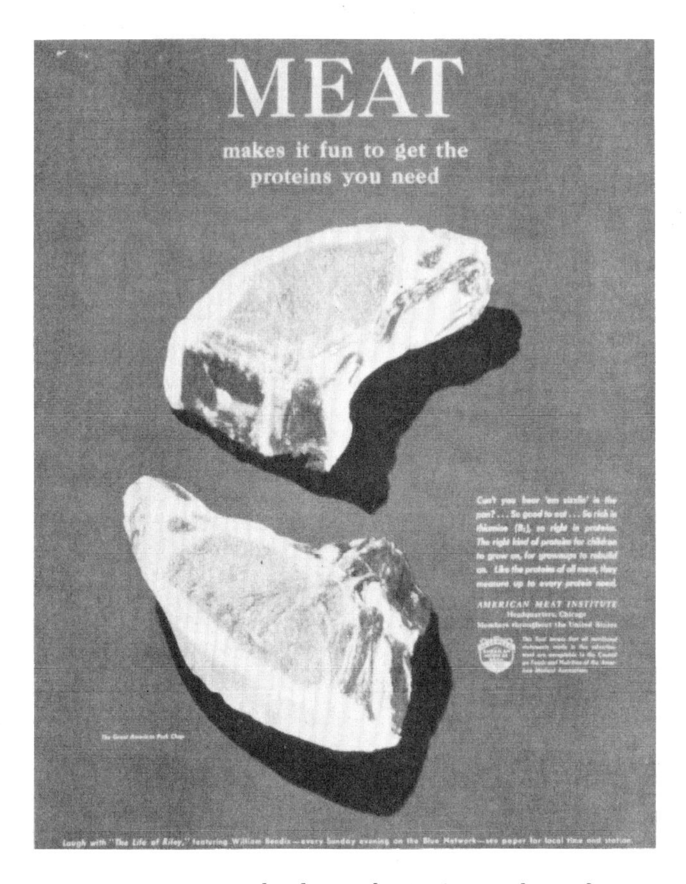

TO TITILLATE APPETITE—*The idea for this 1945 meat ad started, says Mr. Burnett, like this: "I was in Hi Williams' studio in New York and I said, I wonder what would happen if you put a piece of red meat on a red background. Would it disappear, or would it be dramatic? Let's try it." He did. Result: A long campaign of "red on red" bleed ads. Says Mr. Burnett: "This was inherent drama in its purest form, which we try to find without getting too kooky or too clever or too humorous or too anything—it's just natural."*

I had at least acquired facility for putting words together and . . .

Q. *Organizing facts?*

A. Organizing facts and finding things that were most interesting to people. So there I was with Homer McKee. But in the meantime, when I first went to Indianapolis with LaFayette, Earle Howard gave me the job of selecting an advertising agency. I looked through about a year's issues of *The Saturday Evening Post*—which was the leading magazine in those days—and picked out the ads that appealed most to me on the basis of my own judgment—such as it was at that time—on the basis of what I learned from MacManus and others.

During my period at Cadillac, I had joined all the advertising clubs and read all the advertising journals. I had tried to improve myself in advertising quite diligently. So against what judgment I had, I went through *The Saturday Evening Post* and tore out the ads that appealed to me most. I discovered that quite a sizable number of them had been done by Erwin Wasey in Chicago.

Far more had been done by Erwin Wasey than any other agency in the country. This was good enough for me. So I said to myself: "Well, if these people can produce advertising like that, this is what I want." I didn't know anything about them, you understand, I just knew the name of the company and that they were in Chicago. So one Saturday morning, I went over to Chicago—we were still in Detroit; this was before we moved to Indianapolis.

I went to Chicago on a Saturday morning—this was in 1920, I guess. Even then, offices were operating with skeleton staffs on Saturdays, because I walked into the Erwin Wasey offices in the Garland Building and there was nobody in the reception room. And I finally nailed a kid who was walking through and asked if Mr. Erwin was there. He said, no, Mr. Erwin didn't come down on Saturdays. I said, is Mr. Wasey here? He said, no, Mr. Wasey doesn't come down on Saturdays. I said who is here who can talk business? And he said, "Well, our copy chief, Art Kudner, is working back there and maybe he'd talk to you." So this was my meeting with Art Kudner.

Q. *Copywriters were working Saturdays even in those days . . .*

A. Yes. And this was a big account—I mean, it looked potentially very big—it looked like maybe a $2,000,000 account, based on our intended budget, which was very big in those days. I walked into Art Kudner's office, introduced myself, told him who I was. I said, "Would you take this account?" He said, "We sure would!" So I spent the rest of the day with him; we had lunch together and I got acquainted with Art. I found him banging the typewriter in his office—he was copy chief then. I later discovered that Obie Winters —I didn't know this at the time, and this had had no influence on my selection—but Obie Winters, who had gotten me to Detroit, gotten me in the automobile business, had just come to work for Erwin Wasey from Green, Fulton & Cunningham. And so it was a reunion with Obie. And, additionally, getting acquainted with Art.

Erwin Wasey was all in Chicago in those days. It was a very happy arrangement; they did some great work for LaFayette. I was in the middle of that, and I learned a lot from Art, as well as from Obie and others at Erwin Wasey. Then I went to work for Homer McKee after I left LaFayette and Art told me when I left: If you ever are interested in a job, get in touch with me.

Q. *Were you writing copy as an ad manager or editing it?*

A. Oh, I was writing some. But then, of course, at Homer McKee, I wrote a great deal. But shortly after I went to Homer McKee, we got the Marmon account, which was a big thing in those days—now extinct, but it was a fine car in those days. So finally, I stayed in Indianapolis about ten years and had a very happy life there—my three children were born there.

Homer McKee was a fine, thriving agency. But things started going bad with Marmon, due to a change of management and one thing or another. In the meantime, we'd had a thing called the stock market crash in '29 and things weren't too rosy generally. We had a very comfortable life in Indianapolis and a nice home there and everything. But I talked it over with my wife. At my age—I was 40—I thought I'd better get the hell out of Indianapolis if I was ever going to amount to anything in the ad business. So I called Art on the phone. In the meantime, Erwin Wasey had moved their main offices to New York.

I had seen Art over the years; from time to time I had dropped in to see him—Art and Obie both. But I called Art in New York. I said: "I don't know whether you will remember this, but years ago you told me if I was ever interested in a job with you or with your agency, to talk to you." And I said: "I'm doing that very thing—this is a helluva time to do it." He said: "That's just great with me; I meant it at the time, I mean it now; you go to work for our office in Chicago; and I'll get in touch with Chet Faust (who was running the shop at that time) and you go to work there as soon as you can; and you work salary and stuff out with Chet."

So I went over to Chicago and went to work for Erwin Wasey; I was put in charge of their creative work there. It was there that I first got acquainted with some of the people who later joined me. Shortly after joining Erwin Wasey I persuaded them to hire Dewitt (Jack) O'Kieffe, a brilliant writer who had worked for me in Indianapolis. He, of course, was one of those who joined me when we started our own shop in 1935 and is now senior vice-president of our company.

Q. *During that time, in those early days of writing advertising, you worked—from what you said—mainly on so-called hard goods or automotive accounts. Now, after all your years of experience, do you think it's more difficult to write copy for one product over another? Like an automobile over a refrigerator, say?*

A. No, I don't think it makes very much difference. I think if you find the right appeal in a product—one that you can focus on—you can develop it on any product. I know in the experience of our own

"On some types of products—drug products, for example . . . experience is highly desirable—knowing what's worked and what hasn't worked, and knowing some of the scientific facts involved . . . But that knowledge and experience aren't nearly as important as [a writer's] expressiveness, his ability to think and to marshal his thoughts into persuasive English."

agency, some of our best successes have been in industries that I knew nothing about, or our agency didn't know anything about until we started with them. We knew nothing about the railroad business until we got the Santa Fe account. We knew nothing about the petroleum business until we got Pure Oil. We knew nothing about the shoe business and so we got the Brown Shoe Co. account. We knew nothing about the food business until at Erwin Wasey I started learning about the food business, about the Green Giant Co.—and was responsible for all the Green Giant advertising, practically from the time it started. We redesigned the giant as he is today and we've had the account since the very beginning.

Q. *What about the individual copywriter? You see in Advertising Age and the Chicago Trib and elsewhere—you see ads for copywriters with experience on a specific type of product. Do you think a copywriter must have experience in a certain area?*

A. No, not generally speaking. On some types of products—drug products, for example, I think a background of information and experience is highly desirable—knowing what's worked and what hasn't worked, and knowing some of the scientific facts that are involved. Then I think in the food business it is desirable for a writer to have some basic knowledge of nutrition. But that knowledge and experience aren't nearly as important as his expressiveness, his ability to think and to marshal his thoughts into persuasive English. These things he can learn.

But there are some instances where specialized knowledge is desirable. There are certain types of agricultural products where some background is desirable.

Q. *What do you think a copywriter should read? What's your own taste in reading—you read biography and . . . ?*

A. Well, almost everything. I don't have time to do a great deal of reading now; my wife and I are studying Spanish—sort of a hobby—and most of my leisure hours are spent studying Spanish.

Q. *You still do a lot of writing at the shop?*

A. Well, not a great deal—not a great deal that appears in finished form in advertising. I do a great deal of guiding. I write a lot of briefing memos, listing a lot of thought-starting ideas to provoke and stimulate others around the place.

We're going through that process right now on Gallo wine. We had a meeting yesterday of 30 or 40 of us all afternoon—a briefing session on wine, looking at everything that had been done and all the background, the research we had all boiled down. Out of that I'm going to take this weekend to write a memo to all of our creative section. We are going to stir up the creative juices of the whole place, you see, to be brought to bear on it. We often do that when a special problem comes along. When something new comes along, everybody likes to get into the act; and we give them all an opportunity, regardless of who has the final responsibility for it.

Q. *That's one of the things that I also wanted to ask—there are several schools of thought about how you stir up an individual's creative juices. Some writers put their feet on the table and stare out the window with a glass of beer in their hand. Do you have any specific approaches to the problem? From a copywriter's point of view? Do you have any rituals you follow, any special methods?*

A. No. My technique, if I have one, is to saturate myself with knowledge of the product. I believe in good depth-interviewing where I come realistically face to face with the people I am trying to sell. I try to get a picture in my mind of the kind of people they are—how they use this product, and what it is—they don't often tell you in so many words—but what it is that actually motivates them to buy something or to interest them in something.

Q. *In all the years you have been in this business, Mr. Burnett, you've talked with many people and you've edited many pieces of copy from many different writers. Have you ever discerned any thread winding its way through all these people? Do you see any qualities common to all of them? Or do you think copywriters are made up of all sorts and all types?*

A. Well, I think they come from all sorts of places and are made up of all types, but I think among the best ones there's a flair for expression, of putting known and believable things into new relationships. We try to be—which I think typifies the Chicago school of advertising, if there is one, and I think there is one—we try to be more straightforward without being flatfooted. We try to be warm without being mawkish.

I believe that today visibility, sheer visibility, is more important than it's been, speaking of printed advertising—and that applies to television, of course, too. Sheer visibility is important with today's rising advertising costs; if you don't get noticed, you don't have anything. You just have to be noticed, but the art is in getting noticed naturally without screaming or without tricks . . .

Q. *Putting eyepatches on fire hydrants . . . ?*

A. Obvious tricks, yes. Of course we, over and over again, stress this so-called inherent drama of things because there's usually something there, almost always something there, if you can find the thing about that product that keeps it in the marketplace. There must be something about it that made the manufacturer make it in the first place. Something about it that makes people continue to buy it . . . capturing that, and then taking that thing—whatever it is—and making the thing itself arresting rather than through relying on tricks to do it. I mean whether it's a big cake or . . .

Q. *Or an automobile?*

A. Or an automobile. I remember years ago we had a great success when the meat industry was advertising through the American Meat Institute, which was one of the big landmarks in our agency.

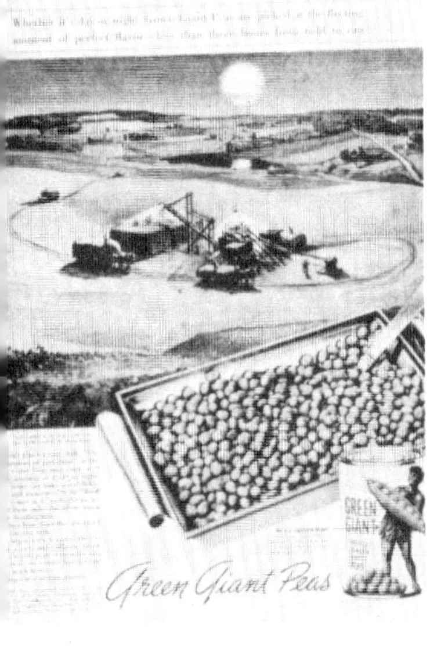

ROMANCED—*This ad in the late '30s for Green Giant Co. (then Minnesota Valley Canning Co.) was written by Mr. Burnett, who said, "It would have been easy to say, 'Packed Fresh,' in the headline, but 'Harvested in the Moonlight' had both news value and romance, and connoted a special kind of care which was unusual to find in a can of peas."*

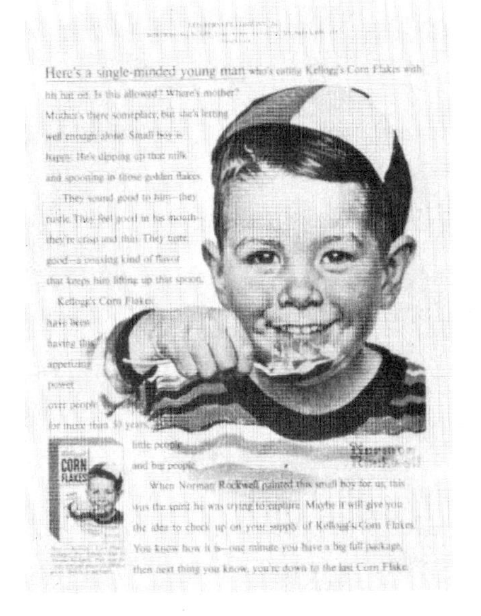

ROCKWELL PERSUADED—*Leo Burnett is credited with the concept (but not the copy) for this series in 1964. He personally went to Arlington, Vt., to persuade a reluctant Norman Rockwell to paint a series of children's heads for use on packages of Kellogg's Corn Flakes. Mr. Burnett's argument: The Rockwell style would get more exposure than ever before. It did.*

We convinced ourselves that the image of meat should be a virile one, best expressed in red meat. A lot of people in the industry said you can't show red meat—uncooked meat—it's distasteful.

But we argued to the contrary, and we did quite a lot of research which showed it wasn't distasteful to women at all. We felt that there is nothing like a piece of red meat to say "meat." So, right from the beginning, we showed a lot of red meat.

But then we went a step further, and this came about more or less by accident. I was in a studio myself one day, the tag end of the day, and we had taken a lot of pictures for ads. At that time I was very active; then we were quite small and a very small group of us did the ads together.

I was in Hi Williams' studio here in New York and I said, I wonder what would happen if you put a piece of red meat on a red background: Would it disappear or would it be dramatic? Run it as a bleed ad—this was before television—and I said, well, let's try it and find out. This was after five o'clock, but we had meat around the place we had been using for other pictures and cooking it and so on, recipes and what have you. So we took a round steak and slapped it on a piece of big red cardboard, and Hi photographed it. We took a couple of pork chops and put them on a red background and photographed that; and some frankfurters and put them on a red background and photographed that.

Later he sent me the prints on these things, and they were terrific, you know. So we chopped them down to size for a bleed page, and took them to the next committee meeting of the Meat Institute. And, boy, everybody cheered and said *give us that!* Well, this was inherent drama, you know. This was drama without any tricks. I mean, the red background was a trick; red against red was a trick, but it was a natural thing to do. It just intensified the red concept and the virility and everything else we were trying to express about meat. We ran those red background ads a long time.

This was inherent drama in its purest form, which we try to find without getting too kooky or too clever or too humorous or too anything—it's just natural.

Q. *I have just one quick question for you. And that is: David Ogilvy says that he heard—we were talking about using vernacular and expressions like "Winston tastes good 'like' a cigaret should" and all that—he said that you are alleged to have a little box in your desk or on your desk, and when you run across a new figure of speech or an expression that strikes you as smart or unusual or off-beat, you write it down . . .*

A. I have a great big folder—and it's getting bigger all the time—in the lower left-hand corner of my desk. I've had it for as long as I can remember, ever since I started the agency, and I call it "Corny Language." Whenever I hear a phrase in conversation or any place which strikes me as being particularly apt in expressing an idea or bringing it to life or accentuating the smell of it, the looks of it or anything else—or expressing any kind of an idea—I scribble it down and stick it in there.

Then about three or four times a year, I run through there and throw a lot of stuff out and pick out things which seem to me to apply to some of the work that is going on in the shop and write a memo about it. So my ear is always tuned for putting usual things in unusual relationships that get attention and aptly express an idea. I call this Corny Language, and I have always done that.

I also have another file which is a bulging one—Ads Worth Saving—which I've had for some 25 years. So I go through them . . .

Q. *Your own and others?*

A. Others—I go through magazines every week. I read the *New York Times* every morning, as well as the Chicago papers, the *Wall Street Journal*—and I rip out ads that for one reason or another strike me as being effective communications, either in the manner of their presentation or in the headline or for some other reason. And about twice a year, I riffle through that file—not with the idea of copying anything but it's apt to trigger something that could apply to something else that we're doing.

"A writer should be joyous, an optimist . . .
Anything that implies rejection of life is wrong for a writer."

George Gribbin

George Gribbin's office at 285 Madison Ave. is decorated in muted browns and reds, furnished in a tasteful mixture of English provincial and American colonial, and brightened with sculpture and photographs of his large family. He has a corner office on the sixth floor of the building, and as he sits cross-legged in a leather wingchair, you have to strain to hear what he says above the taxi horns, shouts, truck and bus exhausts and general din of Madison Ave. directly below . . .

Q. *Mr. Gribbin, how did you come to be a copywriter?*

A. I had gone to journalism school at the University of Wisconsin and I was a pretty good student, and in my sophomore year, I figured that I would rather go on and study English, say. I went on to Stanford and got an A.B. in English. I came back to Detroit and expected they would be very anxious to get me on a newspaper. They weren't.

Q. *What did you do then?*

A. I was so damned innocent about the ad business that I didn't realize there were people in the business of writing advertising and getting paid for it. But a friend of mine suggested I write advertising, so I set out to get a job. I called on some of the Detroit agencies—Campbell-Ewald was one, I remember—but I couldn't get past the receptionist. But I did go down to J. L. Hudson, which is a very big department store—one of the very biggest in the world—and I finally landed a job there because in those days there weren't many people with college degrees applying for department store jobs. And I happened to have been a Phi Beta Kappa.

Q. *That shocked them, I suppose?*

A. Yes. Well, they figured I was soundly educated, so I finally landed a job there. But for a while I thought I was going to be selling Fuller brushes.

Q. *Did you take the job as a stopgap, against the day you could get a newspaper job?*

A. I would guess that I felt that way. Not on a conscious level, but I think for a number of years I always weighed whether I wanted to be a newspaper man, rather than an advertising man.

Q. *Backtracking a bit. What made you want to be a newspaper man? Was your father in the business?*

A. All kids have a great desire to be excellent at something, and I was always lousily coordinated, and was never any good at football, or baseball, or basketball, or other things a boy in high school wants to do well at. So I gravitated toward books, more than would be normal; reading a lot, I think I developed more writing skill than I normally would have. I won a couple of local essay contests, and that gave me the delusion that I had considerable writing ability. I think I overestimated that, though.

Q. *Well, sir, you did get into advertising and you became a very successful copywriter, and that leads me to ask you this question: In your opinion, what kind of training best qualifies a person for success as a copywriter?*

A. Do you mean beginning copywriters?

Q. *No. Copywriters, generally.*

A. Well, I probably won't answer that question directly. In the early days, when I was instrumental in hiring writers for Y&R (I don't do that anymore; I leave it to the copy department) I always felt that you wanted a writer first and a business man second, if you had to choose between the two. I think that you can make a good business man, which a copywriter needs to be, out of a writer, but I don't think you can make a writer out of a business man. I'm somewhat prejudiced that way because I can look back upon myself and say I made it. Now as to qualities, I think that a writer is usually better if he hasn't made a good normal "fit" into living as a younger person.

Q. *What do you mean by that? Would you expand on that?*

A. I mean that I think central to good writing of advertising, or anything else, is a person who has developed an understanding of people, an insight into them, a sympathy toward them. I think that that develops more sharply when the writer has not had an easy adjustment to living. So that they have themselves felt the need for understanding, the need for sympathy, and can therefore see that need in other people.

Q. *When you say "easy adjustment," you mean both economically and psychologically?*

A. I mean psychologically. Although I do feel that there is something of a remoteness from what motivates normal people if you've been brought up in a very rich and protected house. I see no advantage in poverty over a middle-class upbringing, but I see an advantage in middle-class upbringing over a rich one.

Q. *Then you recommend that your writers eat in a Chock Full O' Nuts restaurant once in a while?*

A. I would say that you would be very silly not to eat there once in a while. Not only because it's well to know there are lots of people who are not spending ten dollars for their lunch or dinner, but also because the food's very good. [Laughter]

Q. *Mr. Gribbin, in your opinion, is writing advertising more difficult or less difficult than other forms of writing?*

A. I bring to that question a highly subjective viewpoint, because I've done very little writing except the writing of advertising. But as I measure it against my college experience in writing for newspapers, I believe it is a more difficult craft than journalism, say.

But when you measure a really fine newspaper writer—let's say a Jimmy Reston—against advertising writers, it is possibly more difficult to do the highest order of journalism, than the highest order of advertising. That kind of interpretive writing—the kind done by a Reston or a Walter Lippman, say—requires a more extensive knowledge than the knowledge required to present a product.

Q. *A weightier intellect?*

A. I don't know whether it is a weightier intellect, but you certainly have to know more things about the situation in the Congo, than about a can of soup. However, when it comes to writing a good ad for a can of soup, it's more difficult to do that than it is to go out on an automobile accident, or a robbery, because a car accident and a robbery are interesting to people. It requires no ingenuity to make those stories interesting. It does require great ingenuity to get people interested in the many products that are advertised today.

Q. *What about the brevity necessary in writing copy? You recall somebody's line about needing more time to write a short speech than a longer one.*

A. Of course, condensation is part of the difficulty in writing copy. I think the larger difficulty is to draw upon your experience in living and what you have read, so that you are able by association, by something you know will interest people, to get that product into that field of association. This requires an ability to think up pictures that will attract attention, as well as writing headlines and copy that will attract people's attention. Just putting a bar of soap as the picture in an advertisment, let's say, will not make very many people want to look at that ad. You've got to think of some situation that creates a more interesting picture. And of course this requires a very special kind of searching mind to create these images.

"I think that someone who has never written an ad on an automobile in his life can write a good ad on an automobile."

"There is something of a remoteness from what motivates normal people if you've been brought up in a very rich and protected house. I see no advantage in poverty over a middle-class upbringing. But I see an advantage in middle-class upbringing over a rich one."

Q. *What you are saying, in part, Mr. Gribbin, is that advertising copywriters must also take a very active part in directing the kinds of art in an ad?*

A. Oh, he should always be working with an art man. In my days of writing for magazines, newspapers or posters, I always worked with artists—one of the very best is Jack Anthony—and we never did ads separately. Jack and I used to sit down in the same office and both dream up picture situations, and both write headlines.

Q. *You say your "days of copywriting." How much copywriting do you do now?*

A. Very little.

Q. *Do you do any at all?*

A. I occasionally have ideas for advertisements. And now and then, I feel I can better a headline. But in the main, too much work goes through this shop for me to be classified actively as a copywriter.

FAVORED—*Of ads written by George Gribbin, this is one of his favorites, and demonstrates his credo: "While I can't tell you a ritual to go through [to write an ad], I can damn well tell you a ritual to go through after you do it. Will the headline make you want to read the first sentence of copy, and will the first sentence of copy make you want to read the second sentence? You go straight through the copy. It ought to be at the very last word when the reader wants to drop off."*

My friend, Joe Holmes, is now a horse

JOE ALWAYS SAID when he died he'd like to become a horse.

One day Joe died.

Early this May I saw a horse that looked like Joe drawing a milk wagon.

I sneaked up to him and whispered, "Is it you, Joe?"

He said, "Yes, and am I happy!"

I said, "Why?"

He said, "I am now wearing a comfortable collar for the first time in my life. My shirt collars always used to shrink and murder me. In fact, one choked me to death. That is why I died!"

"Goodness, Joe," I exclaimed, "Why didn't you tell me about your shirts sooner? I would have told you about Arrow shirts. *They never shrink out of perfect fit.* Not even the oxfords."

"G'wan," said Joe. "Oxford's the worst shrinker of all!"

"Maybe," I replied, "but not *Gordon*, the Arrow oxford. I know. I'm wearing one. It's Sanforized-Shrunk—can't shrink even 1%! Besides, it has Arrow's unique Mitoga tailored fit! And," I said reaching a crescendo, "Gordon costs only $2!"

"Swell," said Joe. "My boss needs a shirt like that. I'll tell him about Gordon. Maybe he'll give me an extra quart of oats. And, gosh, do I love oats!"

If it hasn't an Arrow Label, it isn't an Arrow Shirt

ARROW SHIRTS

Sanforized-Shrunk — a new shirt free if one shrinks out of fit

Q. *About having ideas, Mr. Gribbin. Many books have been written and speeches given about techniques for creating ideas. Do you have any comments about this? Do you have a definite technique that you use when posed with a problem of advertising copy?*

A. When I was actively writing copy, I don't think I had a ritual, but I had certain habits. One, I think the writer should get to know a great deal about a product—not just the physical characteristics of the product he is advertising—but knowing the kinds of people who are buying it, and what their motives are apt to be for buying it. To know your prospect and know your product—and know both in considerable depth. From then on, I'm afraid I never had a formula.

I used to get together with a good art man, and we would think of what kind of picture we wanted, what situation. It wasn't pictures separated from copy, it was all mixed together. Going back to a very brief ad I wrote many years ago for Arrow shirts, I think I can illustrate this point. I had felt that just ordinary guys, not the very doggy looking models used in clothing ads, but men like you and me, were the people you were selling shirts to. And I felt if you could convey this point, it would make a good advertisement. So I thought up a headline, which was: "Even I look good in an Arrow shirt." And I felt that we ought to have a really ordinary looking man—and perhaps caricature him a bit. Anthony was wiser—he thought that, yes, it was a good idea—but he had the wisdom that the guy ought to be sort of a Norman Rockwell type, freckle-face young man. Homely, but not caricature.

Now that advertisement does have an idea in it, does have a picture in it, does have a headline in it—and they are all mixed up together, and this is the way I think advertising comes out. It cannot be blocked off into separate pieces. Now, once an advertisement is done, then you can start analyzing it, and very often improve it. While I can't tell you of a ritual to go through to do it, I can damn well tell you a ritual to go through after you do it. Will the headline make you want to read the first sentence of copy, and will the first sentence of copy make you want to read the second sentence? And you go right straight through the piece of copy. It ought to be at the very last word when the reader wants to drop off.

Q. *What and who has influenced you as a copywriter?*

A. I think I was influenced by a number of surpassingly good advertising people. Roy Whittier, Raymond Rubicam, Sid Ward, Ted Patrick, a number of others.

Q. *What did you learn from them?*

A. It wasn't watching them. Y&R has always had a system of copy supervision. No copy goes through the shop without submission to a supervisor. We don't believe that you're the best possible judge of your own baby.

Q. *Suppose you're the top man?*

A. Take it to somebody who isn't the top man and have him look at it. There are a lot of people who have good judgment who are not the top men.

Q. *The people who influence you, do they influence you in a way that you can talk about or simply by osmosis?*

A. I'll give you Raymond Rubicam as hardly a characteristic example because he was better than the rest of us. And everybody in the shop realized it. There was nobody in the place who thought he was better than Raymond Rubicam.

Q. *As a writer?*

A. As a writer, as an adman. And when you worked with Ray, you realized not only that he was very imaginative and exceptionally gifted in his scope but that he was very, very thorough. You were apt to re-do an ad after discussing it with Rubicam anywhere from

WHEN I WAS 28, I thought I'd probably never get married.

I'd always been over-tall, and my hands and feet were always getting in my way, and my clothes never looked nice on me the way clothes looked on other girls.

It seemed pretty certain that no knight would ever come along on his big white charger and carry *me* away.

But a man did come along. Everett wasn't the masterful kind you dream about when you're sixteen, but a shy and awkward sort of fellow who didn't exactly know what to do with *his* hands and *his* feet, either.

He saw something in me that I didn't know I had myself. I actually began to feel like somebody. In fact, both of us did. Pretty soon, we got so used to each other that we felt lost when we weren't together, so we figured it probably was the sort of love you read about in the story books, and we got married.

It was a day in April, and the apple trees were in blossom, and the whole earth smelt sweet. That was nearly 30 years ago and it's been that way almost every day since.

I can't believe so many years have gone by. They just carried Ev and me along so peacefully, like a canoe on a quiet river, that you didn't realize you were moving. We never went to Europe. We never even went to California. I guess we didn't need to, for home was big enough for us.

I wish we'd had children. But we couldn't. I was like Sarah in the Bible, only the Good Lord didn't work a miracle for me. Perhaps He thought that Everett was

Well, Ev died two years ago last April and smilingly, just as he had lived. T trees were in blossom and the earth ag sweet. I felt too numb to cry.

When my brother came in to help me s out Ev's affairs, I found he'd been thou I suppose men built like him always ar wasn't a great deal in the bank, but ther insurance policy that will take care o needs as long as I live.

I'm as content as a woman can be wh she really loved has gone.

Moral: Insure in The Travelers. The Insurance Company, The Travelers I Company, The Travelers Fire Insura pany, Hartford, Connecticut.

three, four, up to 15 to 20 times before he would say it was good enough. And I recollect doing a series of advertisements with him one time which were pointing out the excellence, first of all, of newspapers; then, of magazines; and finally, of the radio networks (it was in the days before tv)—a series of three ads. I wrote the ad for newspapers first.

Q. *These were institutional?*

A. Institutional ads for Y&R. House ads. I wrote the first ad, promoting newspapers, and I brought it to Rubicam and he did what you should always do as a good supervisor. He read the ad through entirely without any comment. He didn't read it part way and then start commenting on it. He read it all the way through. And then he said, "George, this isn't bad, but let's start figuring what there is that might be wrong about it.

"Now here we are running an ad by Y&R that tells the people"—this ad was to run in New York newspapers, full page—"tells the people how much newspapers mean to them in their daily lives. But it isn't just the ordinary reader of this newspaper that we've got to think of. We've got to think what is the reaction of the reporter on the newspaper who reads this. Let's go through and look at it from the reporter's point of view." We then went through it from the

FAVORITE—*This ad without headline for Travelers Insurance Co. is termed by George Gribbin as "the finest ad I ever wrote." He added: "It came right out of my own experience. When my wife was 28 she did not think she was ever going to get married. She thought that she was tall and awkward and nobody probably was ever going to ask her. And this ad went on to the fact that she had been asked . . . married . . . lived a happy life and her husband had died and left insurance."*

publisher's point of view. We went through it from the standpoint of someone who was on a competitive medium. What would the radio people, what would the magazine people think—how would they react to this? What would a stockholder in a newspaper think about it? What would an adman who was reading this ad think about it? Y&R, after all, is signing this.

We went through and thought of everyone you could think of as having a particularized reaction to this ad and saw whether it was right for them. Now there were certain things that weren't exactly right for them but they needed to be said; but you didn't do it carelessly and sloppily. You went through this from the reaction of a linotype operator, a man who delivered the newspapers on the trucks, the reporter, the editorial writers, the competitors—you

"I don't think if [our sons] go to a particular college—let's say, to Yale—that there's something special about a Yale man . . . If the smart place for them to go this year is West Hampton, they ought to go to Rutherford, N. J., too. Education should teach a man to weigh things by himself and for himself, and for the people who are dear to him."

name it, and when you went at advertising this way, you were thorough and you did a lot better advertising.

This was characteristic of Rubicam. And all of us who worked here—my bosses, the Whittiers, the Wards, the Patricks. They've gone through this same schooling. So it was sort of second nature to us to do advertising; thinking about it thoroughly and, if you will, broadly and deeply. You don't get away at Y&R with writing a headline. You sit down and you write 10, 15, 40 headlines out of which you pick two or three that seem to you to be the best, and from these you try to pick out the one that is best of all. But then you go into a supervisor and he says, "Well, I don't know that that's a very good headline, Grib. What other ways did you do it?"

Q. *Then thoroughness, you say, is a characteristic of the exceptional writer of advertising. In your time as a copywriter and a major executive of an agency, have you determined any other characteristics of outstanding creative people? Can you spot these things in people?*

A. Yes. The first thing that marks a good writer is that he avoids the cliché. He avoids the cliché in his speech, not just in his writing. He is careful of not using the hagridden figures of speech in his conversation. If he has a figure of speech that pops out of his mouth, it is more likely to have some originality in the phrasing of it, or he won't use a figure of speech. Another mark of a good adman (not just writers, but everybody connected with the creation of the ad): He will be a widely read person.

Q. *What kind of reading do you do, Mr. Gribbin? What kind did you do when you were actively a copywriter?*

A. I would say I read fundamentally classics, more than the popular fiction of the moment, although any time a person is living there is some outstandingly fine writing going on and the bulk of it will be known to you when you read the book review sections. But you'll find that you'll have friends who run across old books that aren't very well known and if you know that they are discriminating they may set you into reading different things from what you might normally do. I have always been interested in biology and botany. I like to read in that field. I think one of the finest books written in recent years in this country is Donald Culross Peattie's—better check on the exact title of this—but it is roughly "Trees of Eastern and Southern North America." And then he has another one on trees of the western U.S. I just mention that. Our good writers—they may be reading in the field of horticulture as well as the fields of general interest.

Q. *But you do think a writer should read things not related to the business?*

A. Oh, yes. He should be far more than a business reader and a reader of the weekly and monthly magazines.

Q. *I remember writing a report of a speech you made which impressed me at the time, about the "Advertising Renaissance Man" and I think the point was—*

A. Yes, it was one of the points that was made: I think there should be broad reading and I think each person will naturally get into his own esoteric fields of reading.

Q. *But advertising ideas, from the point of view of the copywriter, can come from within and without the business world?*

A. Yes. And a great many of them come out of your own life.

Q. *Incidentally, in your time as a writer, what impresses you now as the finest ad you have written? You're associated with the Arrow ad. Is that your favorite?*

A. I think the finest ad I ever wrote was one for Travelers. And it originally went up to the then president of Travelers with a headline called, "The Widow." And he felt that there was something sort of depressing about the idea of having a headline called, "The Widow," but he liked the illustration and he liked the copy. And he let us set the first sentence of the copy in blackface, or in bold type, and it was a better headline than "The Widow." The headline was, "When I was 28 I thought I'd never get married." [A later version dropped even the boldface—simply an ad without headline.] And it showed a picture of a woman, oh in her 60s, standing on a porch looking at the moonlight. But I think that was the best ad I ever wrote and that came right out of my own experience.

Q. *When you were 28 you thought you were never—*

A. No, no. When my wife was 28 she did not think she was ever going to get married. She thought that she was tall and awkward and nobody probably was ever going to ask her. And this advertisement went on to the fact that she had been asked, she had married, she had lived a happy life and her husband had died, and he was a sort of a thoughtful man who had left her with insurance.

Q. *When did you write that ad?*

A. Probably 25 years ago.

Q. *There are certain disciplines that one must follow in writing, and in life, of course. Do you find it is easier to write with ground rules established either by yourself or by the client, or to write under a carte blanche?*

A. Well, your product, your problem sets certain ground rules for you. You immediately have your ground rules set by having to offer to the reader—or the viewer, in case it's tv; or the listener, in case it's radio—a benefit of some sort in the product or service you're advertising.

Q. *You think you can write good advertising with sacred cows established by the client?*

A. Well, yes, I would say yes, as long as the cow isn't the size of an elephant. [Laughter.]

Q. *We talked earlier about influences. Leo Burnett, I understand, has a little box on his desk and when he comes across a figure of speech, or a piece of vernacular that he likes or that appears new, he writes it down and pops it into the box. Now I have two questions related to this box of Mr. Burnett's: (1) What do you think about the use of vernacular in writing advertising such as "Winston tastes good like a cigaret should?" and (2) do you have a box anywhere around?*

A. Well, I don't have a box. I wish I had known about that earlier. That's a very good idea of Leo's.

Q. *How do you file away your ideas?*

A. I don't file them away. Let's say in the days when I was actively writing copy, or supervising copy, when I had an idea on a product I'd put it down. I didn't have a box. But I used to have yellow pads . . . there was always enough need for fresh ideas, so you didn't have to have an attic full of unused ideas for a particular product. They were hard enough to come by, so they managed to get themselves used with some dispatch.

On the use of vernacular? The American language is a good, salty, homespun, colorful language. And it is that way because of the vernacular. There's just nothing like pieces of the vernacular in advertising, or in any other kind of writing. It's not just using the vernacular, it's using the color of the life around you in a fresh way.

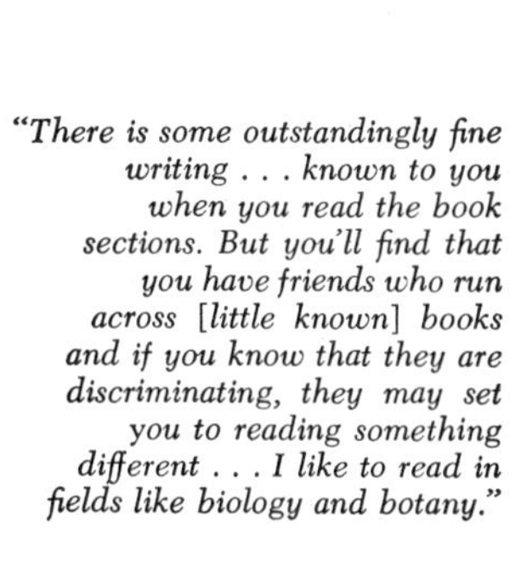

"There is some outstandingly fine writing . . . known to you when you read the book sections. But you'll find that you have friends who run across [little known] books and if you know that they are discriminating, they may set you to reading something different . . . I like to read in fields like biology and botany."

Q. *Let's refine that last question a little. A lot of people say that while a word or phrase might be used frequently, that does not mean the word is proper, or correct. What we mean is the "misuse" of the language in advertising.*

A. You want to get back to the "Winston tastes good" ad?

Q. *Yes, but we don't want to single that out specifically as the glaring offender. It's simply an example of misusing the language.*

A. Yes, now take that phrase, "like," instead of "as." It's just that to a writer's ear, he knows that that phrase has more bite with the word, "like," than with the word, "as." "As" is grammatically correct, and I would tend to use it in conversation.

But many people misuse the word in their language, so "like" is more familiar to their ears. Therefore, use it. There will be times when you will be better off and get more emphasis when you say, "He don't" instead of "he doesn't." In the early days of J. L. Hudson, there was a copy editor whose name was Albert Conkey and he was a former professor of English at the University of Michigan. When he answered the phone and somebody asked him, "Is that you, Al?" he said, "It's me." He felt "It's I" was stilted. And "It's

I" would be stilted in advertising and it would be wrong in many cases to use it, grammatical as it may be. I occasionally get letters from someone who has caught Y&R in a grammatical lapse and I in general feel we don't have to worry about that pedantic attitude.

Q. *About the use of the word "creativity," Mr. Gribbin. Do you have a definition in your own mind about its application in the ad business?*

A. I'm inclined to escape the word, creative, by saying a man is an art man, or a copy man, or a tv commercial man, rather than he is a "creative" man. I've said enough times from the platform that the word, "creative," runs through the entire agency. You can be as creative in media and contact, say, as copy and art.

"I brought the ad to Raymond Rubicam and he did what a good supervisor always should do. He didn't read it part way and start commenting. He read it all the way through. Then he said, 'George, this isn't bad, but let's start figuring what might be wrong'."

Q. *Do you think certain products are easier to write about than others?*

A. Oh, yes. Appliances, for instance, are easier to write about than proprietary drugs. The prospect near the time of purchase of major appliances is very interested in how to invest $150 to $200, and wants to learn all about the product. Nobody is interested in learning about a headache remedy. You have to use considerably more imagination when you're selling this kind of product.

Q. *What about products you prefer to write about. Do you have favorite categories?*

A. Yes, I always like to write insurance copy. But I think in the main I've enjoyed writing about all kinds of products because they tax your ingenuity in so many different ways. One of the great joys in the advertising business, in a large agency, at least, is that you have many different products and problems to which you have to apply yourself. And it's a happy circumstance to have to jump from one product to another.

Q. *You've seen ads asking for writers with experience in one specific product category or another. What do you think about this sort of specialization?*

A. Well, I was made the head of the tv commercial department in the days when there were very few television writers—when tv was still new. So I'm not one to believe that you need to have a background of experience in a particular medium, or particular spectrum of the advertising business. I think that someone who has never written an advertisement on an automobile in his life can write a good ad on an automobile.

Q. *Provided he knows the product he's writing about.*

A. Well, he damned well better find out about it. Just as he should find out about any other product. But I do think there are certain people who have the kind of pictorial imagination and who may be better as tv writers than others who cannot visualize so handily people in motion. After all, there are Arthur Millers who can do a good drama, and there are awfully good novelists—such as Thomas Wolfe—who couldn't write very good plays. There is that ability and I don't think you can suppose it doesn't exist in the man who hasn't tried it.

Q. *Mr. Gribbin, if you had a son who wanted to get into the ad business as a writer, what would you tell him.*

A. Assuming he had writing talent? Well, I would say there are relatively few occupations today in which you can have more hours of happiness than writing advertising copy.

Q. *Returning to my earlier question, Mr. Gribbin. I asked you if you had discerned any specific traits, characteristics, in people who do good copy. You mentioned they avoid cliches . . .*

A. And they read broadly. I think they should participate in life broadly. I think they should do many things. I think they are better off to travel, than stay at home. I think they tend to violate a considerable number of conventions, rather than to subscribe to them. Let them subscribe to conventions after they have decided on their own whether there is wisdom there for them. I don't think that if they go to a particular college—let's say, that they go to Yale—that there's something special about a Yale man. I don't think that if it's better this particular year to wear a three-button, notched-lapel jacket, that they should say that I should wear a three-button, notched-lapel jacket.

I think that, if the smart place for them to go this year is West Hampton, they ought to go to Rutherford, N. J., too. I think that education should teach a man to weigh things by himself and for himself, and for the people that are dear to him.

I have to resort to a cliché here. I think that a writer should avoid stuffiness like the plague. I think he's better off to be a questioner,

"You don't get away at Y&R with writing a headline. You sit down and you write 10, 15, 40 headlines out of which you pick two or three that seem best, and from these you pick the best of all."

than an accepter. I think a good writer can never be a snob; a snob sets himself apart from people, rather than being one of them. That's suicidal for a writer. I think a writer should be joyous, and an optimist, rather than a cynic. Anything that implies rejection of life is wrong for a writer, and cynicism is rejection of life. I would say participate, participate, participate.

*"Many people—and I think I am one of them—are more productive when they've had a little to drink.
I find if I drink two or three brandies, I'm far better able to write."*

David Ogilvy

David Ogilvy opens the door to his old brownstone house on New York's 84th St. and, moving slowly and painfully, ushers his visitor into a sitting room in the rear of the house. The room is furnished in the manner of an English town house. Two walls are covered with bright tiers of books, many of them in their dust jackets, while a third side supports three oil paintings and a handsomely manteled fireplace.

Mr. Ogilvy explains that he has been home from the office for several days with an assortment of "minor ailments," including a sore back and a virus. "Like Job, I suffer at least three afflictions," he apologizes wryly. "Why don't we sit over here?"

The agency man leads the visitor across the room to a wide, flat desk by high French windows. Outside is a bleak landscape of narrow city yards. The desk is strewn with a litter of papers, pencils, odds and ends, a wide ash tray for the scorched Ogilvy pipe, and assorted corporate confetti sent over from his agency. Half buried in the pile is a copy of the expatriated Scotsman's best-selling "Confessions of an Advertising Man." Mr. Ogilvy motions for his visitor to be seated and then, like a man immersing himself in a hot bath, he lowers himself into his desk chair. The interview begins . . .

Q. *A lot of people have talked about devising formulas for creating ideas. Have you such a formula?*

A. Well, we have had a few ideas and I've also got the rudiments of a method for getting the ideas, so I suppose I have to say yes.

Q. *Do you think advertising writing is more difficult than other kinds of factual writing?*

A. One of the difficult things about writing advertising copy is that it is so short. Print ads are short and tv commercials are short. You can't write much more than 100 words in a tv commercial, and that in itself, the brevity of the form, doesn't make it any easier to do. If you've written a lot of advertisements, you train yourself to write very short and tight, so if you try to write a longer thing it's difficult to do.

Q. *Have you ever tried?*

A. I wrote a book a couple of years ago—I wanted to see if I could—there was a matter of some doubt in my mind, and when I had written 800 words I had just about finished the book. Then I had to sit down and learn to write longer. Of course, some very good writers have tried their hands at writing advertising and have failed. Marquand tried to write advertisements and so did Stephen Vincent Benet. And then Hemingway and Shaw tried it and they couldn't do it. Of course, it isn't every competent writer who wants to write ads in the first place. Writing good advertisements is very difficult indeed. But writing good anything is very difficult. I think it was Aldous Huxley who said it is easier to write a passable sonnet than a passable advertisement. I couldn't write a sonnet to save my life, so that's not the case with me.

Q. *Generally speaking, would you rather write ads with "ground rules" established by the advertiser, or by your plans board, or whomever? Or would you rather have carte blanche?*

A. I couldn't write anything without ground rules, but I must confess I prefer to make my own ground rules. We're getting more and more ground rules in the writing of advertising as the corpus of knowledge builds up. I know much more today about how to write good advertising than I did 25 years ago, partly because I studied the subject and partly because so much research has been done about what makes an effective advertisement in any medium. I don't see how you can write anything without a good deal of discipline, and we're getting more and more of that discipline.

Q. *Is this discipline self-imposed? Or imposed from the outside?*

A. Both. I am in a rather fortunate position in some ways, because I didn't write my first advertisement until I was 39. Before I became a copywriter, I was in the research business—I worked with Dr. Gallup in Princeton—and I did a great deal of research. So I approached advertising from the viewpoint of the researcher. In the early days of our agency, I was the research director (among other things) and I used to write research memoranda to myself, to the copywriter, on a Friday. On Monday morning I would come into the office, read the memo, and have to write the advertisement related to the research.

So you see, I fought this battle, as it were, within myself. But of course, that doesn't mean that if you have all the research, all the ground rules, all the directives, all the data—it doesn't mean the ad is written. Then you've got to close the door and write something—that is the moment of truth which we all try to postpone as long as possible.

Q. *Why do you say that?*

A. I suppose with every passing year it gets harder for me to write any advertisement, because I never think I can do it. Sometimes I do write quite a good ad, but whenever I'm faced with having to do one, I have absolutely no confidence in myself at all, and feel sure that I'm going to fail, that I'm never going to have an idea, and that I'm not going to be able to do it. This is quite a serious block. It's made worse for me because I've written some quite well-known advertisements, and I love reading in the press about what a good copywriter I am. But that creates quite a problem for me because I think I used to be a very good copywriter—very good, but I don't think I'm nearly as good today and I don't think I can live up to my record.

Q. *You once described yourself as an "extinct volcano." I believe that was the phrase you used.*

A. Yes, it was.

Q. *Why do you think of yourself that way? And why do you think you're losing your touch?*

A. Well, first of all, it's a fact that while I may not be completely extinct, I'm not erupting with the frequency that I used to erupt [laughter]. I look back longingly on a period of about seven years when I was a real gusher of good ideas—I had good ideas all the time—quite a lot of them found their way into print, and some went into advertising history. Seems to me looking back at those days that I was a very fertile writer, but I'm not nearly so fertile today. I like to comfort myself by pretending that the reason is that I'm too preoccupied with management responsibilities and that I have no *time* for good ideas. But that's really bunkum. I just don't have them . . . But I do, sometimes . . .

Q. *Do you have the time?*

A. I really have plenty of time to have lots of ideas and do lots of copywriting, but I don't do it because I can't do it so well as I used

TIME . . . *"I sometimes have been able to write some good ads by getting up at five or six o'clock in the morning and working through to breakfast."*

to—or so frequently. There are various reasons for this. One is, when I started off copywriting at the age of 39, I didn't know nearly as much as I know now about advertising; I was less disciplined and it was more or less a case of "a fool rushing in where angels fear to tread." Also, I didn't know the conventions that arise out of research. Therefore, I did a lot of work that was original. I didn't know enough to be unoriginal. But the main thing is most copywriters, including me, are better in their 30s than they are in their 40s and better in their 40s than they are in their 50s. It is very, very rare for a copywriter to remain fertile after he's 50—and I'm 53.

[*Mr. Ogilvy paused here and blew his nose in a red handkerchief of the sort one usually sees knotted around the neck of an Apache Indian. Under his conservatively-cut grey tweed suit he wore bright red suspenders to match.*]

Mind you, there are some things you can do, and I do, to try and loosen yourself up if you've got to write an advertisement or get some ideas for some ads or tv commercials, and you feel empty or sterile and uninventive. There are some things you can do about it. Many people, and I think I'm one of them, are more productive and more fertile when they've had a little to drink. I find if I drink two or three brandies, or a good bottle of claret, I'm far better able to write. I also find that if I listen to music, this loosens me up. I also find if I read the "Oxford Dictionary of Quotations" for 15 minutes, this may start trains of thought.

Q. *Some writers have little rituals they perform before writing—like putting on a railroad conductor's cap, for instance, and staring out a window before starting to write. You mention music and one or two brandies as aids in starting the creative juices flowing. Do you use these devices in a ritualistic way, at all?*

A. No, I don't as a ritual. By the way, I'm entirely unable to write anything—even so much as a simple letter—in my office. All I seem to be able to do is answer the telephone, have meetings, and look at other people's work. If I have to do some writing, I have to do it at home here in my house. At nights, or on weekends or in the early mornings. I sometimes have been able to write some good ads by getting up at five or six o'clock and working through to breakfast. Mind you, for some years now I've been head of an agency and not really employed primarily as a working copywriter. We've got 50 working copywriters in our agency today and I have to be very careful. I suppose one of my chief jobs is to get good writing out of other people, and if I frequently enter the fray myself, and write a campaign, I'm placing myself in competition with one of the writers in the agency, and this doesn't have a very good effect on that writer.

[*At this point, Mr. Ogilvy digressed a little, to comment about award-winning copywriters and their reputations.*]

Of course, by the time you win an award like the Hall of Fame, you have got to be well known as a writer. That generally means that you have had to graduate from the copy department into management and have got your name on the door, or else become famous in the advertising business for some reason besides writing. And I think you'll find, in talking to most of the people who have won this award, that they are not really copywriters any more (if indeed, we ever were). I like to pretend I'm a copywriter and if you look me up in that reference work, "Who's Who in Advertising," where everybody gets the chance to write his own biography, you'll see I list myself not as David Ogilvy, "chairman of the board," but as "David Ogilvy, copywriter." I like to pretend I'm a copywriter and I hope I still am, after a fashion.

ONE OUT OF 26—"*When I wrote that ad for Rolls-Royce, I wrote 26 different headlines for it and then got half a dozen other writers from the agency to go over them and pick out the best one.*"

"At 60 miles an hour the loudest noise in this new Rolls-Royce comes from the electric clock"

What makes Rolls-Royce the best car in the world? "There is really no magic about it—it is merely patient attention to detail," says an eminent Rolls-Royce engineer.

1. "At 60 miles an hour the loudest noise comes from the electric clock," reports the Technical Editor of [illegible]. The silence of the engine is uncanny. Three mufflers tune out sound frequencies—acoustically.

2. Every Rolls-Royce engine is run for seven hours at full throttle before installation, and each car is test-driven for hundreds of miles over varying road surfaces.

3. The Rolls-Royce is designed as an owner-driven car. It is eighteen inches shorter than the largest domestic cars.

4. The car has power steering, power brakes and automatic gear-shift. It is very easy to drive and to park. No chauffeur required.

5. There is no metal-to-metal contact between the body of the car and the chassis frame—except for the speedometer drive. The entire body is insulated and undersealed.

6. The finished car spends a week in the final test-shop, being fine-tuned. Here it is subjected to ninety-eight separate ordeals. For example, the engineers use a stethoscope to listen for axle-whine.

7. The Rolls-Royce is guaranteed for three years. With a new network of dealers and parts-depots from Coast to Coast, service is no longer any problem.

8. The famous Rolls-Royce radiator has never been changed, except that when Sir Henry Royce died in 1933 the monogram RR was changed from red to black.

9. The coachwork is given five coats of primer paint, and hand rubbed between each coat, before fourteen coats of finishing paint go on.

10. By moving a switch on the steering column, you can adjust the shock-absorbers to suit road conditions. (The lack of fatigue in driving this car is remarkable.)

11. Another switch defrosts the rear window, by heating a network of 1360 invisible wires in the glass. There are two separate ventilating systems, so that you can ride in comfort with all the windows closed. Air conditioning is optional.

12. The seats are upholstered with eight hides of English leather—enough to make 128 pairs of soft shoes.

13. A picnic table, veneered in French walnut, slides out from under the dash. Two more swing out behind the front seats.

14. You can get such optional extras as an Espresso coffee-making machine, a dictating machine, a bed, hot and cold water for washing, an electric razor.

15. You can lubricate the entire chassis by simply pushing a pedal from the driver's seat. A gauge on the dash shows the level of oil in the crankcase.

16. Gasoline consumption is remarkably low and there is no need to use premium gas, a happy economy.

17. There are two separate systems of power brakes, hydraulic and mechanical. The Rolls-Royce is a very safe car—and also a very lively car. It cruises serenely at eighty-five. Top speed is in excess of 100 m.p.h.

18. Rolls-Royce engineers make periodic visits to inspect owners' motor cars and advise on service.

ROLLS-ROYCE AND BENTLEY

19. The Bentley is made by Rolls-Royce. Except for the radiators, they are identical motor cars, manufactured by the same engineers in the same works. The Bentley costs $300 less, because its radiator is simpler to make. People who feel diffident about driving a Rolls-Royce can buy a Bentley.

PRICE. The car illustrated in this advertisement—f.o.b. principal port of entry—costs $13,550.

If you would like the rewarding experience of driving a Rolls-Royce or Bentley, get in touch with our dealer. His name is on the bottom of this page. Rolls-Royce Inc., 10 Rockefeller Plaza, New York, N.Y.

JET ENGINES AND THE FUTURE

Certain airlines have chosen Rolls-Royce turbo-jets for their Boeing 707's and Douglas DC8's. Rolls-Royce prop-jets are in the Vickers Viscount, the Fairchild F-27 and the Grumman Gulfstream.

Rolls-Royce engines power more than half the turbo-jet and prop-jet airliners supplied to or on order for world airlines.

Rolls-Royce now employ 42,000 people and the company's engineering experience does not stop at motor cars and jet engines. There are Rolls-Royce diesel and gasoline engines for many other applications.

The huge research and development resources of the company are now at work on many projects for the future, including nuclear and rocket propulsion.

By the way, there's another thing that happens to me and no doubt happens to other people in my position: We are constantly being given credit for advertisements which came out of our agencies that we have had nothing to do with. Someone will say, "Isn't that a marvelous ad. Who did it?" And somebody will answer, "Ogilvy." Or "Burnett." or "Bernbach." Well, what do they mean? What do they know? Nine times out of ten I personally didn't do it, nor, I expect, did Leo or Grib or Bill Bernbach. It was done by somebody in our agency, and this makes me feel like an awful fraud. Somebody who takes credit for other people's ideas. I don't do it on purpose, but it does happen in the course of events and I wish I knew how to stop it.

And sometimes, I'm beginning to think, too, that when you become the head of an agency, perhaps you'd better stop writing advertising completely. Raymond Rubicam, who was an extremely good copywriter, told me, in the early days of our agency, that I should never write another advertisement as long as I live. That I should leave that to others. And he could just be right.

[*Mr. Ogilvy stood up gingerly, moved slowly across the room, savagely jabbed a smouldering log in the grate, returned and lowered himself back into his chair.*]

I am . . . uh . . . rather depressed at the moment because I wrote an ad about a month ago that I thought was a very good one. I took a lot of trouble with it and stayed up half the night writing it, and I thought it was an absolute smash. And now it's been presented to the client and it hasn't been okayed and it's beginning to dawn on me that it's not going to be okayed and it's not going to run. I suppose this is something that most copywriters have to get used to and have to live with every day. But it's quite a novel experience with me because I think I can say that up to this point every ad I've ever written has run, which I like. This one hasn't run and I guess isn't going to. And this makes me wonder whether I really ought to go on writing.

Q. *Do you think it's not going to run because it's too good or too bad?*

A. It's just because the client thinks it's not appropriate to his company. And it may be that he's right. I can't possibly judge. Nobody can judge his own work. Incidentally, whenever I do write ads, I never submit them to the client, or allow them to be submitted to the client, until they have been heavily edited by at least one other person. For example, when I wrote that advertisement for Rolls-Royce, which you may remember, I wrote 26 different headlines for it and then I got half a dozen other writers from the agency to go over them and pick out the best one. Then I wrote the copy [about 3,500 words] and then got three or four other writers to go over it and cut out the dull and obscure parts and reduce it down. I have to sit in judgment on a lot of copywriters' work nowadays and I'm always irritated when they bring me just one headline. Why can't they bring me one dozen, or two dozen? Anyway, I'm unable to judge the quality of my own work and I don't see how any copywriter can. A lot of copywriters think they're good judges of their own work. I know I'm not.

Q. *Mr. Ogilvy, you went into copy from research with definite ideas about what constitutes good copy. Have your ideas changed at all?*

A. My ideas have changed, but not as much as they ought to have done. My ideas about what constitutes good copy, almost all of them, derive from research, not personal opinion. And down through the years I try to keep up to date with research, because from time to time it does throw new light on things. For example, Gallup & Robinson ten years ago told us not to start off a tv commercial with an interrupting device, but to start off selling in the first frame.

Well, I believed this—their evidence seemed to be pretty good—and I practiced it. But some recent research shows that this is no longer true, if it ever was. That it does, in fact, pay to start commercials with an interrupting device. To grab people's attention in the beginning. So you see I have changed there. I haven't changed many of my ideas about what makes a good print advertisement. After all, print advertising has been researched for about 40 years and a good deal is known about it, if you want to look it up, whereas tv has been researched for only about eight years and not much is known about it.

Q. *Who has influenced you as an advertising copywriter?*

A. You're bound to be influenced by personal observation of other people's work. One of the earliest influences on me was Rosser Reeves. When I first came to the U.S. in 1937 I didn't know very much about advertising, although I was quite interested in it and I had a rather highbrow, pretentious, literary view of what makes good advertising. Then I met Rosser, who was then a young copywriter at Blackett, Sample, Hummert. He in turn was under the influence of Duane Jones and Frank Hummert, who were essentially Lord & Thomas, Claude Hopkins men. Rosser explained to me very articulately the philosophy of advertising that was then being practiced with notable distinction by the agency he worked for. I also became interested in agencies which were pursuing readership ratings—notably Young & Rubicam and Kenyon & Eckhardt—and I got *that* kind of influence. They were two different schools of advertising, of course, and it took me a long time to reconcile what I learned from both of them.

Now Puerto Rico Offers 100% Tax Exemption to New Industry

by BEARDSLEY RUML

"We don't want runaway industries" says Governor Muñoz. "But we do seek new and expanding industries." Federal taxes do not apply in Puerto Rico, and the Commonwealth also offers full exemption from local taxes. That is why 317 new plants have been located in Puerto Rico, protected by all the guarantees of the U.S. Constitution.

A recent analysis for one Ohio firm revealed that due to tax exemption and operating economies it will increase its net profit from $187,000 to $442,000 a year by locating its new plant in Puerto Rico.

How Corporate Tax Exemption Boosts Profits

How Dividend Tax Exemption Boosts Income

What About Labor?

"Close to Paradise"

Puerto Rico's Finest Hour

Transportation

Are You Eligible?

Or mail coupon for free booklet.

100% OGILVY—*"I stayed home for ten days and did nothing else but write that ad."*

More recently, I've observed some of the things that Doyle Dane Bernbach does, particularly in print. This is new to me. I don't think they really got it from anybody. They just sort of created an original school out of air. Some of it has impressed me very much. I couldn't write the Volkswagen campaign if I live to be 100, but I admire it very much and it seems to me that it opens new doors.

[*Mr. Ogilvy was interrupted here by the door bell. A messenger delivered a package. Mr. Ogilvy stood by the door of the sitting room for a moment, letting the accumulated smoke from his pipe and the faint odor of the fire in the grate drift out and upwards to the floors above. Then he closed the door and returned to his chair, favoring his sore back as he sat.*]

I've got a fairly well defined creative philosophy, based largely on research. But perhaps it's too well defined. Too restricting. I'm always hoping that one day some young man will come into my office and say, "Your 96 rules for creating good ads are for the birds. They're all based on research that is out of date and irrelevant. Here are 96 new rules based on new research. Throw yours out of the window . . . You're an old dodo, living in the past, move over, I have written a new dogma, a new dialectic, and I am the prophet of the future . . . " I hope this will happen. In some small ways, it's already happening in our agency and this is very fortunate. Sometimes very annoying to me—but very fortunate for the agency.

Q. *Has your method, your style of copywriting, been influenced at all from sources outside of the advertising business? You say you had a "literary, pretentious" view of advertising . . .*

A. When I was a boy I did.

Q. *Has fiction, poetry had any influence . . . ?*

A. No, I don't think so. Perhaps on others it may. I don't read any poetry. I can't bear reading poetry, and I don't read one novel from one year to another. I read other things, but I don't think the stuff I do read has much influence on what I write. I don't think I am a good writer, incidentally, but I do think that what I am is the best damn editor in the world. I can edit anybody well, including myself. So what I do is write my stuff and then edit and edit and edit until it's reasonably passable. At least, it sometimes is. It's a painful business for me. I know other writers who are much more fluent, and facile, and surer-footed, and can write their stuff down, and that's the way it runs. I'm not that good. I'm awfully slow. I've done as many as 19 drafts on a single piece of copy before I've presented it to anybody to edit. I wrote 37 headlines for Sears, Roebuck last week and I think got three that I thought were good enough to submit to other people for their comment. So, you see, the writing business is not easy for me.

Q. *Do you find certain products easier to write about than others?*

A. Yes, I do. I find that products that interest me personally are easier to write about.

Q. *Rolls-Royces interest you, for example?*

A. Yes. The reason we took the Rolls-Royce account is that I've always, ever since I was born almost, had an interest in Rolls-Royce motor cars, and I wanted to try my hand at writing about them. But I can imagine some products I wouldn't be very good a writing about, since I'm not interested in the subject.

Q. *Such as . . . ?*

A. Well, I'm not interested in chemistry. I shouldn't say that because we've got the Shell chemical account, but we've got two or three writers in the agency who are interested in chemistry and can deal with that. I flunked out of Oxford because I couldn't pass the most elementary chemical exam. I'm not interested in it, really. I'm an awful duffer at it. To me, it's an opaque mystery . . . Nor am

I interested in philosophy; I couldn't write anything about philosophy. I am interested in developing nations, generally, and Puerto Rico specifically.

Q. *I think you mentioned once that of all the ads you've been credited with, an ad for Puerto Rico gave you the most satisfaction.*

A. Yes, I think that was a good ad. It took an awful lot of hard work on my part to write it. I had to read a lot, of course. I stayed home for ten days and did nothing else but write that ad. It was an unspectacular, long-copy ad. I think the headline was, as I recall, "Now Puerto Rico offers 100% tax exemption to new industries."

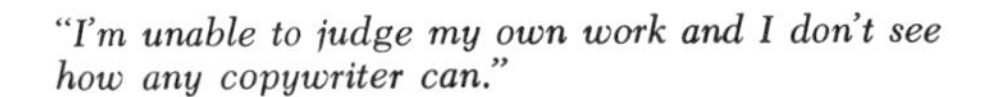

"I'm unable to judge my own work and I don't see how any copywriter can."

And there was a long subhead, with the copy purported to be written by Beardsley Ruml. I was really able to put my heart in that because I was both intellectually and emotionally committed to the subject.

We for some years did the advertising for Helena Rubinstein. I wasn't very good at writing that, myself, because I'm not terribly interested in lipstick and face powder. You see, the posture I always take when I finally close the door and have to write the ad is this: I always pretend that I'm sitting beside a woman at a dinner party, and she asks me for advice about which product she should buy and where she should buy it. So then I write down what I would say to her. I give her the facts, facts, facts. I try to make them interesting, fascinating if possible, and personal—I don't write to the crowd. I try to write from one human being to another human being in the second person, singular. And I try not to bore the poor woman to death, and I try to make it as real and personal as possible. Incidentally, I have a theory that the best ads come from personal experience. Some of the good ones I have done have really come out of the real experience of my life, and somehow this has come over as true and valid and persuasive.

Q. *Could you give me an example?*

A. All right. I wrote an ad that some people think was infamous—for Austin cars, about 15 years ago. The headline was, "I'm sending my son to Groton with the money I've saved driving an Austin." The quote was attributed to an anonymous diplomat. Well, I had just left the staff of the British embassy in Washington and I was the anonymous diplomat. I was driving an Austin because I had a little boy whom I was to put through school, and I was very poor, and I figured if I had an Austin, which was very economical, I would be able to save enough money to send my son to boarding school. It was very true and valid.

But let me get back to what I was saying. It's very difficult for any copywriter to write persuasive copy for a place, or a product, that he's not interested in. Unfortunately, most copywriters aren't in a position to choose their assignments (except the more successful ones, perhaps, who may have some choice in the matter). But when you're the head of an agency you're in the most glorious position, in that you can choose what you work on. But I think when you assign accounts to writers, you should give them accounts that they can get involved in, emotionally, and not assignments that will bore the poor things to death.

What I mean is, I don't think you can *sell* anything unless you quite genuinely feel that you want to persuade people, your own family, your own wife, your friends, the people you meet at dinner parties, the world at large, to use that product. And you can't persuade them to do it unless you genuinely believe it. Good copy can't be written with tongue in cheek, written just for a living. You've got to believe in the product. This may sound corny, but it happens to be the harsh reality.

Q. *Mr. Ogilvy, in your years in the advertising business, and as a supervisor of copy people, have you noted any distinguishing characteristics which enable you to identify the creative man? Apart from his writing, that is.*

A. For 16 years I've been trying to find some common denominators which seem to apply to all good creative people. There aren't any. If I could find five or six characteristics of good creative people, I would of course be more successful in hiring them. I might make up a list and say, curiosity, one; large vocabulary, two; good visual imagery, three, and so on. Then you could interview hundreds of people with those attributes and hire the best of the bunch. But I don't know of any common characteristic. I don't know what kind of education makes a good copywriter.

Claude Hopkins, for example, maintained that nobody with a college education could write an advertisement addressed to the mass millions. That's absolute poppycock. I was almost going to say that hard work is the characteristic of a good copywriter, but I'm not even sure of that. We've got 50 copywriters and I suppose the good ones are the ones who could, at the end of the year, point to one or more really successful campaigns that they have created. I don't know how I can be any more specific than that. The search

The man from Schweppes is here

The man in the Hathaway shirt

MASTER'S TOUCH—*Says Mr. Ogilvy: "Another thing that happens to me and no doubt to others in my position: We are constantly given credit for ads which came out of our agencies that we have had nothing to do with . . . It was done by somebody in our agency, and this makes me feel like an awful fraud. I wish I knew how to stop it." The two ads shown here need raise no such fears—they were written by Mr. Ogilvy, himself.*

"Claude Hopkins maintained that nobody with a college education could write an ad addressed to the mass millions. That's absolute poppycock."

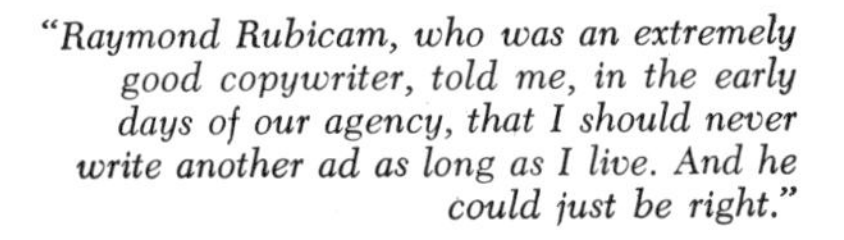

"Raymond Rubicam, who was an extremely good copywriter, told me, in the early days of our agency, that I should never write another ad as long as I live. And he could just be right."

for generalities about how to write copy, and what makes a good copywriter, goes on—and goes on pretty hard in my agency. But I don't know if I've been making any progress.

Q. *What about writers who write well only in tv, and those who write well only in print? Shouldn't a writer be able to write well in both?*

A. There are nowadays quite a lot of fairly good writers who can't write a print ad, at all. We've got some writers in our agency—young ones, who do good tv commercials and that's all they've ever done. You ask them to do a print ad, and two or three days later they bring it in and it isn't an advertisement, at all—it looks as if it had been written by someone who has heard an advertisement described, but who has never actually seen one. But, they are tv writers—it's what they know, it's all they know, and God bless them.

Q. *What about print writers?*

A. Equally, of course, there are a lot of copywriters who have been brought up in print and who've never got interested in writing tv commercials and who can't do it. There are very, very few writers who are equally proficient in both tv and print.

Q. *Do you, yourself, prefer print to tv?*

A. (After a lengthy pause) I'm a better print writer than a tv writer, and to that extent I suppose I prefer print. I could name you three or four print ads I have written in my life that you might recognize and think well of, but I'm terribly afraid that I couldn't name any tv commercial that I've personally written which you would immediately recognize and applaud. You see, by the time tv commercials came along seriously we had already gotten some writers, younger than me, and the tv work seemed to fall to them, rather than me. But I remember about 12 years ago—it seems like 100 years ago—when I was going through my good period, we had very few accounts in those days, even fewer than we do now, and we had 15 separate campaigns going. That was all. And 14 of them were my own personally—all print. Today, I don't know if I could point to any of our campaigns and say, "I wrote that." I rather fancy myself as a print writer, but I don't as a tv writer. We've got 50 copywriters in our agency, and I don't think more than three of them are better print writers than I am. But I think about 37 are better in tv than I am.

Q. *In "The Last Tycoon," a screenwriter tells a character, a novelist, that writing for the screen is "describing," not "writing." The writer doesn't "write" what is on the screen, he "describes" it. Would you agree with that?*

A. A very good description. You see, here's what has happened, one of the reasons tv advertising has been so bad: Before we had tv, we had radio. And radio advertising is words. In the old days of radio, the days of Charlie McCarthy, Fred Allen, soap operas, the *big* radio days, the commercials were 60 seconds of words. Then came tv, and the people who wrote radio commercials started writing tv commercials, and what they wrote was words. And they tried to use words to sell. Then after a bit they discovered it wasn't words that sold, it was pictures. The action. I sometimes think that a good commercial should only have two words in the beginning that said simply, "Watch this." Then show pictures so interesting, so persuasive, that the viewer would have to go out and buy the product.

I'd like to say something further, that isn't exactly relevant to this. If you are a writer of novels, or plays, or poetry, you can write and take your own time, generally speaking. And when you've finished writing six months or six years later, you publish it and that's that. But in advertising, you've got the deadlines, you've got to have the idea, and it's got to be a *great* one, and you've got to have it Tuesday morning. This is not easy, and it makes many of us flop pretty badly. We have to write something good in a hurry and we end up writing something bad in a hurry.

Q. *Is there any way to avoid this?*

A. I sometimes thought if I were an advertiser I would hoard my money and I'd have my agency work to produce a great campaign, great by test, by any standard you wish to apply, and then, by George, I'd pour on the coal, let fly all my accumulated war chest of advertising, instead of dribbling my money away month after month, year after year. Unfortunately, the tax laws don't allow manufacturers to accumulate their advertising money. The real problem is that most advertising copywriters today who are any good—unless like me they've retreated into top management—find themselves having to write a tremendous lot of story boards and ads for a tremendous lot of products under great pressure, and we have to produce far more than any good writer can produce well. We've got to keep the stuff going.

Take this research maw. Some of our clients, quite rightly, I think, refuse to put a commercial on the air unless they've first been tested and then they use the one that tests best. That means that the copywriter on that account has to write not one great commercial, but several—so they can be tested.

Q. *What about the supply of talent?*

A. In most agencies—in all agencies—there's a shortage of copywriters. Good ones. And the good ones are so overworked they almost stagger from one assignment and one meeting to another. They've got to get the stuff out and they've got to get it out by Tuesday afternoon and then they've got to get it okayed. In that kind of atmosphere, it isn't the easiest thing in the world to produce immortal advertising.

Q. *Let me ask you a corny question, Mr. Ogilvy. Knowing what you know about the advertising business, sitting where you sit as head of OBM, suppose you found that your son wanted to go into the business as a copywriter. What advice would you have for him?*

A. To begin with, most sons who want to go into the advertising business today don't want to go into copy. For example, we've got 22 young men in our agency who have come to us from the business schools, Harvard, Columbia, Dartmouth and so on. These 22 young business school graduates are very formidable young men. Not a single one is a copywriter. They've all chosen the account executive side of the business. No, if my son—he's 22—came to me and told me he wanted to come into advertising and be a copywriter, I

"I've done as many as 19 drafts of a single piece of copy. I wrote 37 headlines for Sears, Roebuck last week and I think got three good enough to submit."

would say, "Don't." I would tell him he would start off with serious problems, such as how to get out from under my evil shadow. People would say he's not so good as his daddy, or, he's better than his daddy ever was. Then I would say to him, "You are 22, and I don't think you should be a copywriter unless you've done something else first."

I've seen some men leave college and become copywriters; we've had a few of them, but I think it's difficult. As I said, I wrote my first ad when I was 39, and I really struck it pretty good right off. I couldn't have done it unless I had done a lot of other things first. I had been a door-to-door salesman for kitchen stoves, and I worked in the research business, and I had experience that was enormously important when I sat down to write my first ad. But if my son *insisted* on going into the business, I would tell him to work harder. Before sitting down and writing 39 ill-chosen and vapid adjectives, he should know his product, study it thoroughly. He should read a lot of advertising.

I read a lot of magazines, have for years, but I don't read the editorial, at all. I just read the advertisements. I would advise him to get a job at an agency that had a reasonably high level of quality, where he could learn good discipline, where he would have good leadership. An agency that took a position about what is good advertising and what isn't.

Q. *What about the use of the vernacular in copywriting? The "Winston tastes good like a cigaret should." That kind of usage.*

A. For some reason or other, I never studied English grammar in school. I don't know the rules of grammar. And I keep on hearing people talking about that phrase, "Winston tastes good," as wrong grammar. But I don't know why. It sounds all right to me. And it seems to me that people who see something wrong with that are insufferable pedants. But perhaps I'm just saying that they are grammarians and I'm not.

If you're trying to persuade people to do something, or buy something, it seems to me you should use their language, the language they use every day, the language in which they think. We try to write in the vernacular. Leo Burnett is very good at this. Somebody told me he has a box on his desk in which he puts vernacular phrases every time he comes across one. I'm not very good at this because I'm a foreigner, and I've never had much mastery of American vernacular. And whenever I try it I fall flat on my face. But I do admire it in other people, the ability to write as one human being talks to another, and that means vernacular.

Q. *Just as a point of interest, do you have a "box" in which you file ideas when they occur to you? How do you file away random ideas and thoughts?*

A. I do keep a drawer in my office in which I put things, and I have a pad beside my bed on which I write things in the middle of the night. For years I've been meaning to get a little pocket notebook to write things down in, but I can never remember it. Very inefficient of me.

"No, sir, I'm not saying that charming, witty and warm copy won't sell.
I'm just saying
I've seen thousands of charming, witty campaigns that didn't sell."

Rosser Reeves

ROSSER REEVES has a reputation for arriving for appointments five minutes early. But today he arrives ten minutes late. He is tense as he walks into his office at Ted Bates & Co.; he has had a luncheon meeting with a client, it has gone badly, and he seems preoccupied as he greets his visitor and seats himself on a sofa at one end of the office.

He thumbs idly through a magazine taken from a stack on the coffee table before him and waits while the interviewer fumbles with the tape machine. A cold afternoon sun floods through the corner windows and glints off a large brass and crystal hourglass standing on his desk at the opposite end of the room. Mr. Reeves lights another cigaret and looks at his watch as the interview begins . . .

Q. *What I want to ask you first . . . you went into copywriting with some definite ideas. Have they changed at all?*

A. Not a great deal, no. Slightly, as far as the perfecting techniques of advertising are concerned. But I've been in the business now for 36 years; I started as a copywriter in 1929. What I refer to as the immutable principles of advertising have not changed appreciably in that 36 years.

Q. *The immutable principles of advertising . . . but what about the immutable principles of copy?*

A. Well, I'm talking about the immutable principles of copy. I was coming from Baroque Restaurant three minutes ago to meet you and the Fifth Ave. bus passed me and I saw an example of what I mean by an absolutely ghastly advertisement. It was a big poster on the side of a Fifth Ave. bus; it stopped right in front of me for about a minute and a half, and it had a picture of an absolutely ravishing girl. I think the headline said, "The most startling innovation to come out of Sweden since girls . . . since blondes." And I admired the blonde and as the bus moved on and I walked across the street to meet you, it occurred to me that I don't know what product it was.

Q. *It's Erik cigars, I think.*

A. Erik cigars? Well, I didn't see the name of the product. I was studying the blonde, being human as we all are. Five or six years ago I met a card manipulator named Cardini who was very famous, and he wanted to tuck a half deck of cards into his collar, and as he did it, as his left hand was putting the cards into his collar, he produced a fan of cards from under the knee. Everyone was watching the fan coming from under the knee; they weren't watching the other hand. That's typical of that advertisement on the side of the bus. I had an enchanting picture of an enchanting girl, and I don't know what the product was. Now this to me is a waste of money.

Q. *I think in magicians' parlance that's called misdirection.*

A. Misdirection. I call it in my book vampire video, distraction techniques. It's one of the most common mistakes in advertising today.

Q. *Speaking of misdirection, how did you set out to be a copywriter?*

A. Oh, I liked advertising.

Q. *Were you misdirected into the copy field, or did you plan to get into copywriting, or did you plan to get into some other phase of the business?*

A. I wanted to be a newspaper reporter, because it was the only job I could get at the time, but I wanted to write copy, and I am still a copywriter—a simon-pure copywriter.

Q. *You know, George Gribbin told me he wanted to be a newspaper reporter but he took a job as copywriter against the day he would be a newspaper man.*

A. I wanted to be a newspaper reporter, too, but I was only 19 years old, and I discovered in 1929 or '30 that I could make only $14 a week. My enthusiasm for police reporting dimmed very rapidly at that time.

Q. *You hardly make much more than that now in most places.*

A. Yes, it's a badly paid profession, I'm told, although it's very interesting. My boss at that time, who was city editor of the *Rich-*

SLAMBANG ANACIN—*Said Rosser Reeves of this tv ad: "You can come to me with all the subjective judgments you want, and . . . the artsy-craftsy crowd; I have other criteria . . . A big drug company doesn't spend $86,400,000 unless they're making money on it. That money was spent on one television commercial. It cost $8,200 to produce and it made more money than 'Gone with the Wind'."*

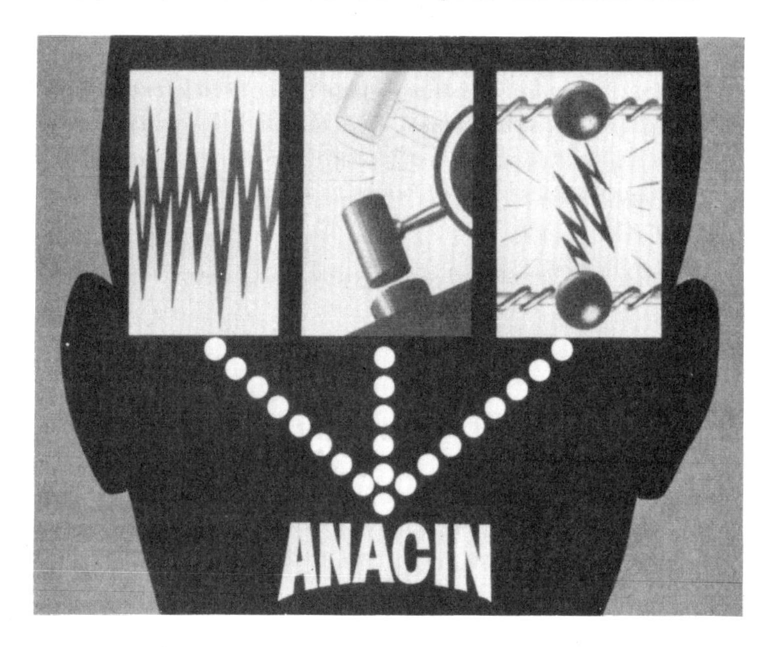

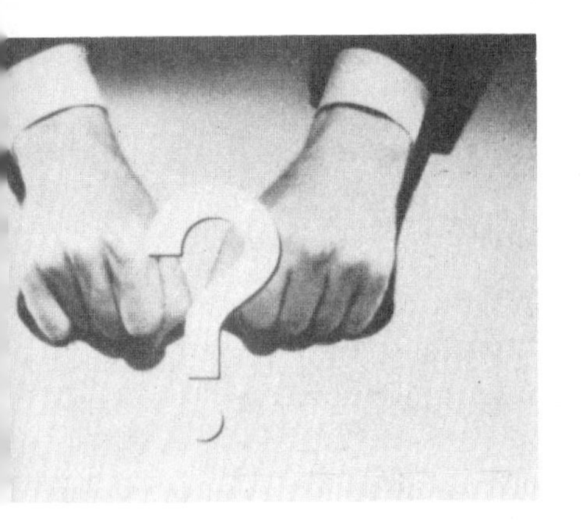

IDEA IN PRODUCT—*Mr. Reeves recalled his first meeting with John MacNamara, president of M&M's Candies: "As I found out after ten minutes' conversation, the advertising idea was inherent in the product. It was the only candy in America that had chocolate surrounded by a sugar shell . . . I put the two hands on the screen and said, 'Which hand has the M&M chocolate candy in it?*

mond Times Dispatch, was named John Denson. Since then he's been editor of *Newsweek,* editor of the *New York Tribune* and is currently editor of the *Journal-American.* In a lunch recently with John, we were debating which was better paid, and he said, "I found the newspaper business very rewarding and very highly paid."

Q. *This touches upon a question I wanted to ask you later and that's about training and background. What do you think, in your years as copywriter and supervisor of people who write copy, what do you think are the best kinds of training a copywriter can have, in advertising?*

A. To work in a big advertising agency under people who know what they're doing.

Q. *From scratch, you mean?*

A. From scratch. Where else can they learn it? It doesn't exist. The advertising business today, despite the courses in advertising—given at various universities—is very much like law was in the time of Henry Clay and Patrick Henry—you know there were no law

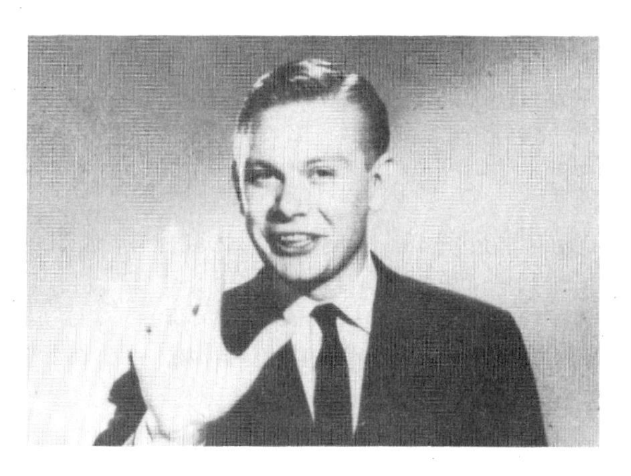

Not this hand that's messy, but this hand because M&M candies melt in your mouth, not in your hand.' That phrase . . . is a technique. But the idea of the campaign, that these candies do not melt because of the sugar shell, was the easiest thing in the world because it was inherent in the product."

schools; you read law under a practicing lawyer. And to learn the copywriting business today you have to read advertising under a practicing advertising man.

Q. *You don't think that a person from the outside, someone from another field, can come in and be a successful and capable copywriter?*

A. Oh, of course not. That's as silly as saying a copywriter could turn to novels; let's say emulate Ernest Hemingway. They're two different things. I'm quite sure Shakespeare would have been a bad copywriter; Hemingway would have been a bad copywriter, Dostoevsky or Tolstoy—you name the novelist. We're discussing two different specialties.

Q. *Do you think a copywriter can learn from any of these other fields? Can he learn from the novelist, can he learn from poetry, can he learn from other fields of writing? As equippage for himself?*

A. Only to this extent. The only connection between a superb novelist like Hemingway—I happen to be a great admirer of Hemingway . . .

Q. *He did write an ad, you know . . .*

A. Yes, I understand, but you know, he didn't write that ad. He wrote a piece of copy that went into the ad. He wasn't an ad-maker. But the only connection between a working novelist like Hemingway and a working copywriter is that they both use the English language.

Q. *You spoke about techniques. There've been lots of books and lots of speeches about techniques—formulas for writing, procedures one follows to get ideas, etc., in copy. Do you have such a technique?*

A. I'm not sure that I understand your question. Most of the speeches and books that I've read along those lines, I consider nonsense. That's like going to Mozart—I'm told that Mozart wrote symphonies at age 12—and saying, "Do you have any formula by which you write symphonies?" Now, you either write symphonies or you don't write symphonies. Within the framework of harmony and the laws and structures of music, the composer has to use certain basic techniques. If you're discussing the difference between one musician who can write a great symphony and one who can't, and you ask him questions about what are his procedures, you're just wasting your time. He doesn't know what his procedures are.

Q. *Some people seem to know what their procedures are. For example . . .*

A. Well, I think you're talking about a different thing. David Ogilvy and I are both disciples of Claude Hopkins, and the procedures you're talking about . . . it's not how we arrive at ideas, but it's the technical way that we work out the ad after the idea has been arrived at.

Q. *Well, arriving at an idea itself is the most difficult accomplishment. This is one of the continuing problems of a man who's faced with creating an idea, say for an insurance company year after year, month in, month out . . .*

A. It's either one of the most difficult things in the business to do, or it's one of the easiest things in the business to do, and it depends on your product. For example, in 1954 two men named Charles White and John MacNamara walked into my office. John was president of M&M's Candies. He said their advertising wasn't suc-

"Let's say you have $1,000,000 tied up in your little company and suddenly your advertising isn't working and sales are going down. And everything depends on it. Your future depends on it, your family's future depends on it, other people's families depend on it . . . Now, what do you want from me? Fine writing? Or do you want to see the goddamned sales curve stop moving down and start moving up?"

ceeding and they needed an idea that would sell. Actually, as I found out after ten minutes' conversation, the advertising idea was inherent *in* the product. It was the only candy in America that had chocolate surrounded by a sugar shell. At this point the idea lies on the table right in front of you. There's no searching for an idea at all. At this point the only problem is how do you take that idea and put it into an ad? Now you enter the realm of technique—which is the way you write an ad, not what you say in the ad. In this particular case, as you know, I put the two hands on the screen and said, "Which hand has the M&M chocolate candy in it? Not this hand that's messy, but this hand because M&M candies melt

"You must make the product interesting, not just make the ad different.

in your mouth, not in your hand." Now, the writing of the phrase, "M&M candies melt in your mouth, not in your hand," is a technique. Perhaps it could have been phrased 15 other ways. But the idea of the campaign, which was to say that these candies do not melt because of the sugar shell was the easiest thing in the world, because it was inherent in the product.

Q. *Do you think that most solutions are in the product?*

A. No, unfortunately not. You get into an enormously interesting area here now. Many, many years ago there were some naive manufacturers who believed that they could bring you a product

And that's what too many of the copywriters in the U.S. today don't yet understand."

that had no appreciable difference over the competitor, and they said, "Write good copy and make it good." Today we know that isn't true. Lever Bros., Procter & Gamble, Colgate, Bristol-Myers, American Home Products, Alberto-Culver—all the big companies—realized that the copywriter is almost helpless unless they build the idea into the product. Once the idea is built into the product, the copywriter doesn't have to search for it. Then he has only a technical job, which is how does he present that most effectively to the public.

Q. *Do you think that copywriting as it's done today is a technical job rather than a craft or an art? Do you think you have to be a technician rather than a craftsman?*

A. You have to be both. Let me come back to the previous point, if I may. John Crichton, when he was editor of ADVERTISING AGE, one day said to me: "If your research and development are only in the typewriter of some copy man, then you are already lost." He's correct. It's absolutely true. The manufacturer should bring the copywriter a product that deserves to be on the market. It should have a point of difference from other products. And that point, the idea behind the campaign, is very, very easy to find. For example, if the manufacturer brings you a motor car that can go 500 miles on a gallon of gas, you don't have to look far for a campaign idea. The idea is right in front of you. If on the other hand, you have an Edsel that's not very different from any other car, you are doomed to failure in advance. I don't believe any copy brilliance could have saved the Edsel.

Q. *You mean phrase-making?*

A. Phrase-making won't save you.

Q. *You've been copywriting since 1929. Do you prefer to write ads for certain types of copy as against others?*

A. Oh, I don't think so. I think an advertising copywriter fundamentally is very much like a general surgeon. One day he has to operate on the liver, the next day it may be an appendectomy, it may be an eye operation the third day, or brain tumor the fourth day, but a well-rounded advertising man has most of these techniques in his kit.

Q. *These are mostly unconscious techniques, then, instinctive, would you say?*

A. No, I don't think they're instinctive at all. A few moments ago I mentioned an advertisement which was, in my opinion, guilty of misdirection. I stared at it for a minute and a half, yet I never saw the name of the product or the picture of the product, and I still don't know whether it was a beer, cigar, or balloon. Now, a knowledge of what is misdirection and what isn't is not instinctive. Far from it! If it were, so many advertising writers would not be practicing misdirection day after day—and lowering the efficiency of their advertising rather than raising it.

Q. *You mentioned novels earlier. Do you write other material at all. In other fields? Poetry? Books?*

A. Yes. I write short stories as a hobby, and poetry.

Q. *Do you think advertising writing is more or less difficult than writing in other fields—in the newspaper business, for example?*

A. I don't think the question means anything. I mean, again as I said, we both use the English language and we're both writers. Well, a weight-lifter uses his muscles, and so does a surgeon and so does a parachutist, but the question begs the issue . . . Advertising is a specialized skill. So is newspaper writing, and so is poetry, and so is the novel, and so is the play. Now a good playwright may not be a good novelist, a good novelist may not be a good poet, all three of them may be lousy newspaper men. You put them all together and none of them may be able to write advertising. On the other hand, you may take a Claude Hopkins or a John

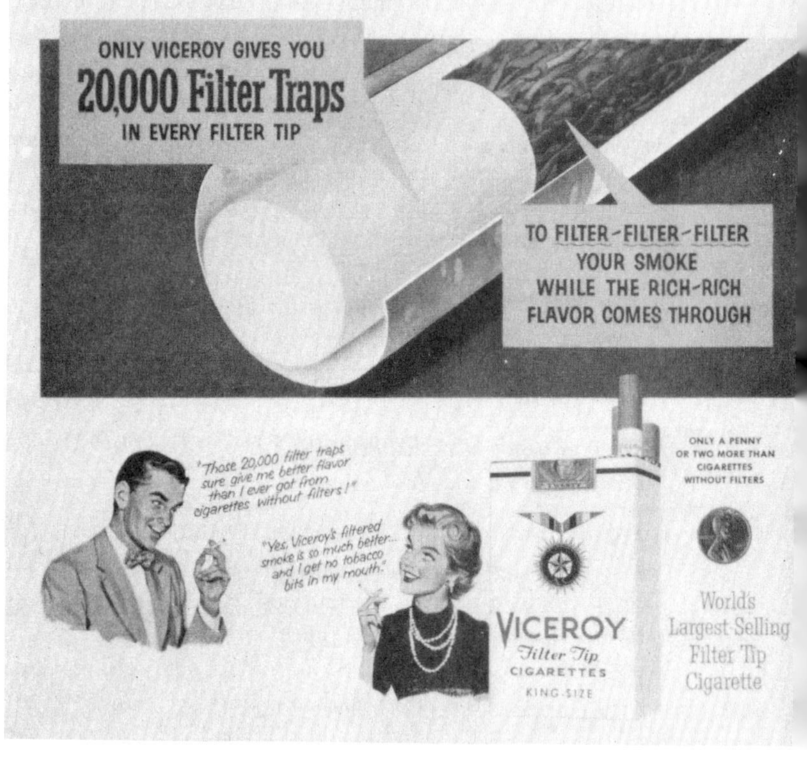

SLEEPER—*In 1945 Mr. Reeves spotted a pack of Viceroys on the president's desk and asked who had the account. The client replied, "Nobody. It's a sleeper—a filter cigaret." He allowed Mr. Reeves to do a campaign for it on $41,000 left over from Kool's production budget. Results: A campaign including this ad. "Six or seven years later," recalled Mr. Reeves, "Viceroy was spending $18,000,000 a year."*

Kennedy or a Rosser Reeves and they may be able to write advertising but they might not be able to write a play like Eugene O'Neill.

Q. *Let me ask you, how much copy do you write now?*

A. I'm still a working copywriter. I think I'm the only chairman of the board that is. I still write copy and still write campaigns, and I think that's my major job. Look, one of my clients, in the last ten years, spent $86,400,000 on one piece of my copy. Just one piece. One piece of copy—$86,400,000! Isn't he entitled to the top talent at this agency or the top people at this agency for $86,400,000? That's an enormous sum of money.

Q. *Who was that, may I ask?*

A. We never talk about our clients.

Q. *O.K. Who edits your stuff? Do you edit your own?*

A. In my position—I'm in the happy position of being my own editor, unless a client interferes, which of course he has a right to do. We are agents and not principals.

Q. *It's interesting you use the word "interferes." This touches upon a question I started to ask you and that is about ground rules. Frequently a client says, "I require that this phrase or this word, this group of words, be in an ad—I require that a certain model be used or a certain situation be used. Write copy around that situation." Do you find it more, or less, difficult—or do you prefer to write with the ground rules established either by the client, or by your plans board or by anybody else?*

A. Clients do establish certain ground rules. By and large, nine out of ten times these are helpful. It's a great mistake to think that the advertising agent knows more about the business than the client himself. I have not found that to be true. The client knows more about his product, more about his company, more about his needs. So they do set up certain ground rules. But nine times out of ten we in the agency set up far more ground rules than the client does.

Q. *The ground rules being your "Unique Selling Proposition"?*

A. No, no. That's an oversimplification. The ground rules in our opinion are what makes good advertising as opposed to what makes bad advertising. For example, we happened to start this conversation with a discussion of what I call distraction techniques—I will not allow distraction techniques in this agency if I can prevent it. And yet, I can sit down any night in front of the television screen and six out of ten of the commercials are so filled with distraction techniques that I am astounded that those companies don't know that they are throwing away their money.

You see, what a copy man often thinks is a brilliant idea in his own subjective judgment can make a terrible advertisement as far as the client is concerned. In my book I said the art of advertising is getting a message into the heads of most people at the lowest possible cost. Now that may often entail the use of techniques that the copywriter might describe as terribly dull. Or he says, "My God. I could write something better than that."

Getting the message into the heads of the most people at the lowest possible cost, well, it's almost a problem in engineering, and we should subordinate our own creative impulses to that one over-all objective: Does this advertisement move an idea from the inside of my head to the inside of the public's head? The most people at the lowest possible cost. What else is this business all about?

Look, a client comes to me and he's in trouble. His brand is going down. Let's say he lost 6% on the Nielsen index. Let's say he's spending $15,000,000 a year. That man is concerned with only one thing. He is not concerned with how the advertisement is written, whether it wins any advertising awards—whether it's an immortal piece of prose, whether it's written in poetry. He wants to get the points back on the Nielsen.

Q. *Which is a technical job.*

A. Of course it's a technical job.

Q. *So, then, you mentioned earlier, at least I understood you to say, that a copywriter must be both a technician and a craftsman, a combination of both?*

A. Your terms confuse me. Let me put it another way: If you were ill, and you went to the Mayo clinic and you did not know what was wrong with you, I don't think you're concerned with whether the surgeon slices from north to south or east to west. You want to know what's wrong with you. You want repairs. You want to be restored to health. Now, too many advertising men forget that this is their basic reason for existing. Some of the greatest copywriters, some of the most *legendary* copywriters in the business are legendary only because they haven't been caught.

Q. *You mentioned you are a disciple of Claude Hopkins. This prompts me to ask you about influences. What influences have you had? You are obviously a very successful copywriter. Who or what has influenced you, aside from Mr. Hopkins?*

A. Look, I'm going to use the medical analogy again. If you went to a doctor and said, why do you take care of your patients the way you do? Who influenced you? He might say that Harvey influenced him, because Harvey discovered the circulation of the blood. He couldn't treat his patients unless he knew about the circulation of the blood. He would be a bad doctor if he didn't. So, I've been influenced by those pioneers of the business. Like Claude Hopkins and John Kennedy who in the early days of this very recent business set down certain basic principles which are not going to change no matter what happens. The blood will circulate. The skeleton is still there within the flesh. And a doctor or surgeon can never depart from those principles. Now this is true in the advertising business, although a great many copywriters don't know it.

"David Ogilvy and I, strangely enough, see almost eye to eye. His techniques are different from mine—I'm more in the drug business than he is. You wouldn't use a drug technique on Hathaway shirts. But if you look at the advertising of the two agencies, you would discover that David and I are operating on the same principles."

Q. *Let me ask you some questions about copywriting, specifically. You frequently see ads in the newspaper for copywriters with package goods experience under 40. Do you think copy skills increase or diminish with age? That there's any relationship at all between accomplishment and age?*

A. That's the kind of question you always get asked in interviews. And I don't think it's an intelligent question. Because again, you can't generalize. I know a surgeon who's now 71 years old and he's still one of the best in the world and people come from all over the world for the ministrations of this one man. No, I don't think a 68-year-old copywriter—I keep coming back to analogy of the surgeon—can write with the kids. That he's as creative. That he's as fresh. But he may be a better surgeon. His ad may not be quite as fresh and glowing as the Madison Ave. fraternity would like to see it be, and yet he might write an ad that will produce five times the sales. And that's the name of the game, isn't it?

Q. *That is. Well, instead of generalizing, let's be a little specific about yourself. Do you think your own skills and abilities have increased with the years? Do you find any diminishment in your ability to produce, at all?*

A. I think you should ask that of other people. I don't think any man—if he's going downhill, can tell it himself. After all, if he's going downhill, then his judgment is on the way downhill.

Q. *Well, how do you keep sharp? You have many magazines on the table here. What do you do when you're not writing copy? How do you recharge the batteries?*

A. I go to Jamaica and lie on the beach. Or I go up to the Manhattan chess club and play chess. Or I go over to "21" and have a scotch and soda. Or I go home and sleep. Or I sail my boat.

Q. *Then let me ask you this. In your years of writing copy, you must have produced ads of which you are inordinately proud—or fond. Not necessarily the most successful, I mean.*

A. I don't think of ads so much as I think of campaigns. When a client comes to me in trouble, and I prepare a campaign for him—not an ad, but a campaign concept—and if over a period of ten years, everything else being equal, because copy is not the only prime mover in this business, and I see his business going up and up and up, I consider that a good campaign.

One of the striking things about the Bates agency is that we are going to bill in this calendar year about $250,000,000. We are having our 25th birthday in December. In that time this agency has lost just one account. Our clients are some of the biggest and most sophisticated companies of the world, in terms of advertising. Our clients live by advertising. I'm refering to people like American Home Products, Standard Brands, British American Tobacco, Colgate-Palmolive, Wilkinson Sword Blades—you know the list.

They don't stay with us because we're incompetent. Here's an agency that in 25 years has become the fifth largest agency in the world and very shortly will become the fourth largest agency in the world. This is not done by salesmanship. By personality. It was done because over that 25 years, in the course of spending billions of dollars for these people, they have found that our advertising works.

Q. *One thing puzzles me. You mentioned earlier that you were confused. Now I'm confused. If I were starting out in the copy business, and had an opportunity to talk to a man like you, a copywriter in a position you hold, I would be very curious about how a guy improves his skills in copywriting. Perhaps to emulate what you've done. Practice what you have practiced. But I get the idea that you feel there is no way for a copywriter to learn from experience in the craft of copywriting. I'm not talking about advertising. I'm talking about copywriting.*

A. Oh, I disagree with you utterly. The creative department of this New York office has a payroll of about five and a half million dollars a year—just for the creative department.

We have a vast number of trainees coming in from France, Germany, England, Japan . . . and each of our copy groups here has one or two trainees attached to it. [*Mr. Reeves, who seems to be a fairly heavy smoker, pauses to light his third cigaret.*] Some brilliant young Radcliffe graduate, *summa cum laude*, will come in and she will write her first television commercial. One I saw last week started with a very well known verse [*Reeves quotes from memory*] . . . "She walks in beauty like the night of cloudless climes and starry skies/and all that's best of dark and bright/meets in her aspect and her eyes."

This was for a deodorant. After she had wasted 50 seconds of the commercial, she discovered in about five minutes that it was no good; that everything she was doing was wrong. The group head ripped it down off the wall and said, "You don't know what you're doing." Yet this girl, inside of a year and a half, will be writing good copy. She'll never dream of starting a commercial like that again, because she'll learn that it's unprofessional. That she doesn't know what she's doing.

So we train them and we train them thoroughly, and they learn it in practice. We're *making* copywriters here all the time. By the dozens.

Q. *Your impatience with artsy-craftsiness is quite evident. So you feel that it's a long and tedious job to learn to write better copy. That you learn by practicing it. That there are no general conclusions you can draw after 30 years in the business.*

A. I didn't say that there weren't any conclusions. I could draw whole encyclopedias full of conclusions. But I don't mean to bore you or bore your readers by sitting here and giving you 122 immutable ways to write a successful ad. I assume that's not what you're here for.

Q. *No. I'm here to find out, for example, if you feel that a guy who can write well in print can also write well in tv. Whether you feel if someone in the copy business should concentrate in one medium or another?*

A. No. I feel that a good copywriter can write print, television or radio. If he's a professional.

Q. *Let me ask you the inevitable question. If you had to give advice to a young chap starting out in the copy business, what would it be?*

A. I would say go to work for one of the great, realistic agencies that understand what they're doing. And learn how they do it. And learn why they do what they do. It's as difficult to become a good copywriter as a good brain surgeon. [*Pause*] Some of the people that float around in this business and are allegedly great copywriters at great salaries, we wouldn't pay $50 a week to at this agency. I think a great many copywriters in this business earn their living because they haven't been caught.

Q. *Caught doing what?*

A. Writing bad advertising.

Q. *The bus poster you mentioned.*

A. That type of thing. As I explained in the first chapter of "Reality in Advertising," it's very difficult in this business to correlate sales with advertising. It's a cliche of the business that if it's a good campaign sales go up, and if it's a bad campaign sales go down. Well, that isn't true. We know that you can run a lousy campaign and sales will go up. You can run a very brilliant campaign and sales can go down—due to other factors in the market.

If I may pursue a medical analogy again, we know that if you go to the doctor it's generally accepted that even if you didn't go, 94% of the people would get well, anyway. And whether or not the

"Only advertising men hold seminars and judge advertising. The public doesn't . . . The public either acts or it doesn't act."

doctor gave them the proper treatment is the question that you're really asking.

There are certain advertising agencies in this business that write types of accounts where the copy is really more paid publicity than it is advertising copy. There are other agencies which handle clients who have to live by advertising. The advertising either works or it doesn't. And you find it out with amazing speed. In this type of agency you learn the advertising business.

Look, you have a competitor called *Madison Avenue.* They get a group of advertising professionals and they pick the best advertising of the year and the worst. [*Mr. Reeves gets up and gets a copy of the publication from his desk. July, 1964.*] And among the worst, they have two of the most successful commercials now on the air. One is the Action bleach by the Bates agency and the other is the white knight by Norman, Craig & Kummel. Now, listen to this [*he reads*]: "Which tv commercials do creative executives personally consider the best and the worst . . ."

[*Mr. Reeves slaps the page with the back of his hand and glares at the visitor.*]

Now, these are "creative executives" and they picked as the worst, two of the most successful commercials now on the air.

[*He reads some more from the publication, quoting the critics who use phrases such as "condescending" and "frightening to the housewife" in describing the Bates-created Action bleach commercial. The commercial features a giant's arm emerging from a washing machine.*]

This to us—and we have the greatest group of professionals here at Bates on Madison Ave.—this to us is garbage; and the only word we have for it is garbage. Now, I read this magazine, and I read your magazine, and nowhere does anybody ever ask the question, how did that commercial work? They're *speculating* on what the housewife thinks. They're speculating on whether it's good or bad. But nobody ever says, let me see the figures. Now isn't this odd?

Q. *It is indeed.*

A. When John Crichton was editor of ADVERTISING AGE, I said to him that somebody, some day, is going to put advertising awards on the proper basis. And that basis is, does it work? The question has never been asked in any advertising award that has been given. And yet look at the panel from what I was just reading. The head of the U.S. Information Agency, the dean of Columbia's graduate school of business administration, the president of the Committee for Economic Development, the president of Smith College, the chairman of a great public relations firm, the presidents of two huge advertising agencies—a total of 25 leading educators, editors, publishers, teachers, public relations and advertising men.

[*Mr. Reeves was referring to a panel formed by the Saturday Review to judge advertising.*]

And they don't know what they're talking about. I can excuse some of these people—they're not professionals. But I find it very difficult to excuse ADVERTISING AGE and *Madison Avenue* and *Printers' Ink*—theoretically, they are trade publications and they should know what they're saying.

Q. *Of course, John E. Kennedy was the gentleman who coined the phrase, "salesmanship in print." Do you think the copywriter is first, a salesman who happens to know how to write, or a writer who happens to know how to sell.*

A. You keep asking me silly questions.

Q. *I don't think it's silly. What I'm asking is, if you think a person who wants to write copy in an agency should be a salesman, first of all, and sharpen his selling tools, rather than a writer, a craftsman, who should concentrate on improving his craft, his writing.*

A. You're discussing opposite sides of the same coin. You're looking at the converse of the same proposition. They call it in mathematics the "reciprocal." If one is true the other has to be true. If he isn't a salesman, he can't write selling copy. If he isn't a writer, he can't be a salesman in print. Because it's inherent in the phrase "advertising writing."

Q. *I think this touches on your objection to these advertising executives who judge advertising competitions. I think they probably feel copywriting is a little more than selling. There's a craft, a beauty, if you like, involved.*

A. Mr. Higgins, let us say that instead of working for ADVERTISING AGE, you had started a company—you name the product. Let's say it's a shaving cream, a frozen food, a razor, an automobile tire—I don't care. And let's say you have $1,000,000 tied up in your little company and suddenly, for reasons unknown to you, your advertising isn't working and your sales are going down. And everything depends on it. Your future depends on it, your family's future depends on it, other people's families depend on it. And you walk in this office and talk to me, and you sit in that chair. Now, what do you want out of me? Fine writing? Do you want masterpieces? Do you want glowing things that can be framed by copywriters? Or do you want to see the goddamned sales curve stop moving down and start moving up. What do you want?

Q. *I think you know what I want.*

A. Well, then, your question answers itself, doesn't it?

Q. *It does, but if you will forgive me, I think you are overlooking one salient point in this. And that is, you do not have to write stuff that is pleasurable to look at, but that can't sell. I think that's the major objection to the arm coming out of the washing machine. It's not very pleasurable to look at. I think you can sell and still write things that are pleasurable to look at.*

A. I don't know, Mr. Higgins, what you consider pleasurable. After all, that's a highly subjective thing. I remember when David Ogilvy got his first drug account. He put on the famous Grecian statues that your magazine week after week said was the most objectionable, offensive commercial ever put on the air. I wrote a letter to David and I said: "You are now in the drug business. If you do it 'correctly,' you are going to be in trouble with ADVERTISING AGE, *Madison Avenue* and *Printers' Ink*. If you do it 'incorrectly' you are going to lose the business." And David wrote back and said, "It's just that simple."

Look, in the course of running a very big operation here, we have made in the course of the last 25 years every conceivable copy experiment for one of our big drug products. I'll take you down right now into our screening room and I will show you—I don't know what you mean by "pleasurable to look at," because I don't know

"It's very difficult to measure, to correlate copy effectiveness with sales. That's particularly true of, let's say, automobiles. But there's one field in which copy correlates exactly, and that's the drug business. Because in the drug business it's a pure copy operation. It's copy and nothing but copy."

what your definition of esthetics is—but I will show the commercials that *worked.* And I will show you 20 others that we wrote for that same product that were so charming, so pleasing, and so delightful. And they failed. Now if you are the manufacturer, what are you going to run?

You know, only advertising men hold seminars and judge advertising. The public doesn't hold seminars and judge advertising. The public either acts or it doesn't act.

If my advertisment gets them to act and your advertisement doesn't get them to act, then I'm going to make that judgment first, and I'll debate with you later whether you find it pleasurable or unpleasurable.

Now, we're not in favor of commercials that are in bad taste, or terribly ugly commercials. But sometimes a commercial that conveys the idea is not what other practitioners of Madison Ave. are looking for. There's nothing particularly beautiful in a tv screen with two fists stuck in the face of the television viewer and you say, "Which hand has the M&M's chocolate candy in it?" That certainly isn't esthetic like the Swedish girl on the bus poster. But they've had to build a new factory—to supply the demand.

Q. *Well, Mr. Reeves, I didn't come here as a critic of any product of any advertising agency. But I'm somewhat aghast that you seem to feel charming, witty and warm copy won't sell.*

A. No, sir, I'm not saying charming, witty and warm copy won't sell. I'm just saying that I've seen thousands of charming, witty campaigns that didn't sell. (*Pause.*) You know, I said earlier that it's very difficult to be able to measure, to correlate copy effectiveness with sales of a brand. That's particularly true of, let's say, automobiles. But there's one field in which copy correlates exactly. And that's in the drug business. Because in the drug business it's a pure copy operation. It's copy and nothing but copy.

Q. *You mean ethical drugs or proprietaries?*

A. Proprietaries. They don't have any salesmen . . . Now, I've picked up *Life* magazine. [*Mr. Reeves holds up a copy of Life, opened to a small space ad for Excedrin.*] It just happens to fall open to an ad for a Bristol-Myers product called Excedrin. Do you find that ad pleasurable? It's a hand holding a bottle.

Q. *No, I don't find it pleasurable, but I don't find it objectionable, either.*

A. Is it witty or charming? Let me read it to you: "Over 31,000,000 people have discovered new Excedrin, the extra strength pain reliever. Tablet for tablet, 50% stronger than aspirin for relief of headache pains . . . "

Q. *I neither find it objectionable, nor do I find it overly stimulating.*

A. Well, I find it overly stimulating, because I write the product that competes with this, and in the last two years I've seen them get 7% of the headache industry business with that ad. You may not find it overly stimulating, but out of the 200,000,000 Americans who have headaches, enough of them do so that 7% of these people are now taking Excedrin. And that to me is the name of the game.

Q. *I'm getting a headache right now* [laughter]. *But seriously, I'm not here as a critic . . .*

A. No, no. I'm just trying to give you an interesting interview. I don't want something to come out over my name with a lot of idle generalities. That's all.

Q. *Well, here's one thing I wanted to ask that certainly isn't general. How did you get into the ad business in the first place?*

A. I went to work as advertising manager for a bank in Richmond, Va., in 1929.

Q. *And from there?*

A. I came to New York and became a copywriter at Cecil, Warwick & Cecil. Now Warwick & Legler. And they fired me. Then I went to Ruthrauff & Ryan for four years.

Q. *Did you land the job at Cecil right away? Did you have any difficulty breaking into advertising?*

A. No, I gave them the bank account in Virginia in return for a job in New York at $34.50 a week.

[*At this point the interview ended. Mr. Reeves lighted another cigaret while his visitor began to collect the equipment in preparation for leaving, The conversation turned to the Copywriters Hall of Fame Awards. The tape machine was still on as the agency man continued to talk . . .*]

You know, there is such nonsense in this business. Recently I received a letter from the head of the Advertising Club in New York. He asked me if I would serve on a panel—another one of these endless panels—to pick good advertising. I wrote him back and I said no, there are too many such panels now, and I thought they did the business more harm than good.

You know, every now and then we hire some bright youngster who has watched the giving of these advertising awards and it takes us about a year to get all of the nonsense out of his head. And I said to him (the Ad Club president) that I do not want to compound the felony, therefore I would not serve on the panel. Two days ago I had a luncheon with the Advertising Writers Assn. of New York, who nominated me . . .

Q. *Do you think it's a step in the right direction? Nominating you to the Hall of Fame? You're the Peck's Bad Boy of the artsy-craftsy crowd in town.*

A. Now, isn't that interesting. That's a nice phrase, "I'm the Peck's Bad Boy of the artsy-craftsy crowd." Well, I'm the Peck's *Good* Boy of the people who want to move the goods off the shelves. But no, they're going to give out gold keys at the Hall of Fame ceremony, and I said I wonder if these people know that when you give them a gold key you're not giving them a gold key because they *have* written a good campaign—but because you *think* they may have written a good campaign. The evidence is not in yet.

If you want the Hall of Fame to be a *true* Hall of Fame, and if in the course of this ceremony you are going to pick great campaigns, then I think you're going to have to go back into history and get some of the immortal copywriters now dead, like Wilbur Ruthrauff, John Kennedy, Claude Hopkins, Sterling Getchell, O. B. Winters, Sid Schwinn—and give *them* gold keys for the great historic campaigns that changed the face of this business, The evidence is all in on these campaigns. They really worked. Their campaigns are monolithic monuments. What you refer to as the artsy-craftsy crowd I refer to as the crowd who are using the wrong criteria in our business.

Q. *Speaking of campaigns, you never did complete your thought about your own favorites.*

A. I'll tell you a campaign that gave me great, great pleasure, indeed. Back in 1945 in Louisville, Ky., I picked up a package of Viceroy cigarets off the desk of the president. And I said, "Who makes these? And he said, "We do." And I said, "Who has the advertising account?" He said, "Nobody—it's a sleeper." I said, "Let me write a campaign for it. It's a filter cigaret—let me see what we can do with it." And he said, "Well, that's fair enough. We have $41,000 left over from our Kool's production budget. I'll give you the $41,000 and let's see what you can do."

So I wrote a campaign called "20,000 tiny filter traps—twice as many as any other brand." Six or seven years later, Viceroy was spending $18,000,000 a year.

Now, I repeat again, that's the name of the game. Therefore, you can come to me with all the subjective judgments you want, and you talk about the artsy-craftsy crowd; I have other criteria, that's all. You take this one piece of copy which I mentioned earlier. A big drug company doesn't spend $86,400,000 unless they're making money on it. That money was spent on one television commercial. It cost $8,200 to produce and it made more money than "Gone with the Wind."

Q. *I wish you would tell me which commercial that was.*

A. It was the Anacin commercial. You know, we look at advertising from one viewpoint, and most of the people in the advertising business look at it from another. David Ogilvy and I, strangely enough, see almost eye to eye. His techniques are different from mine—I'm more in the drug business than he is. You wouldn't use a drug technique on Puerto Rico. You wouldn't use a drug technique on Hathaway shirts. But if you look at the advertising of the two agencies, you would discover that David and I are operating on the same principles.

You take his great Rolls-Royce ad; there was no nonsense about that. In fact, David himself will tell you that he took the campaign almost completely out of three pages in Claude Hopkins' book, "Scientific Advertising." It's only 70 pages long. Read it. You'll find the Rolls-Royce campaign described in detail. How the ad should be written, what it should say—and the book was written in 1925. So you see, David uses the same principles.

So, the summation:

Let's call it the artsy-craftsy crowd. They believe their advertising has to be different. Strangely enough, such writers have a pseudo rationale for just striving after mere difference and they plead it with passionate earnestness. The illogicality of their argument is not obvious to them, and it's even less obvious to the public and to many business men.

In fact, it sounds enormously convincing, and it goes like this: One, the advertising, not the product, must compete with a tremendous number of other advertising messages. Two, therefore the advertisement, not the product, must get attention. Sounds reasonable, doesn't it? Three, therefore a given advertisement, and not the product, must be different.

Such reasoning bypasses the product, and when it does, it bypasses the advertising function. It is a classical example of confusing the means with the end. For if the product is worth paying money for, it is worth paying attention to.

The consumer need not be shocked or entertained into giving his attention. I mentioned the beautiful Swedish girl on the poster. This writer was trying to shock and entertain me into reading about that product and I never saw what that product was. You told me, and I still don't know. I have forgotten already.

I know perfectly well if I were to marry that great classical calendar of a nude Marilyn Monroe to a paint ad it would certainly make a different paint ad, but I would be falling for that false chain of logic I just gave you.

[*During this discussion the agency man opened a copy of Life and read a straightforward piece of copy headed, "Introducing the Latex wall paint with the built-in second coat," for Dutch Boy paints. "I prefer this ad," he said.*]

So, getting back to our earlier discussion about how we train copywriters, one of the things we tell them, one of the first lessons they get is this lesson—you must make the *product* interesting, not just make the ad different. And *that's* what too many of the copywriters in the U.S. today don't yet understand.

For further information or a current catalog, write:
NTC Business Books
a division of *NTC Publishing Group*
4255 West Touhy Avenue
Lincolnwood, Illinois 60646-1975 U.S.A.